As a Condition of Your Freedom

A Guide to Self-Redemption from Societal Oppression

As a Condition of Your Freedom

A Guide to Self-Redemption from Societal Oppression

By Perry Redd

Redd Media Publishing
Washington, DC

ISBN 10: 0615903126
ISBN 13:978-0-615-90312-5 (Redd Media)

Library of Congress Cataloging-in publication
data

Designer: Dawhayne Parker
Art Director: Perry Redd
Editor: Barbara J. Patterson
Production Editor: Perry Redd

To Perri and Kai

Set yourself free...

Contents

Acknowledgements

Foreword

Preface

As a Condition of Your Freedom, You Cannot:

Index

Bibliography

Endnotes

Acknowledgments

Allow me to give thanks where thanks is due. I thank God for embedding a strong desire to see justice done. I only chose to write this book because I heard of the conviction of Nelson Mandela while he served his time at Robben Island. In 1985, he was offered release— his freedom—if he would simply renounce violence. He declined.

He was imprisoned another decade before he was released. I understood that fully. I too had an offer of a complacent condition if I gave up my fight for justice to the government. I declined. As a consequence, they charged me with three additional— greater penalty—crimes. In the end I won, but along the way, I questioned *my* judgment to challenge the one with the most resources and all the cards. I dedicate this writing to Vernon "Shawn" Daniels, whom I met at FCI Edgefield while serving the tail end of a 70-month federal prison sentence. At the release of this printing, he's seven years into a 15-year unjust conviction—after fighting the good fight in a federal court in Tallahassee, Florida; and to Leon Kennedy who fought like a dog while the prison cheated him out of a judge-ordered sentence. To Oscar Cole-El, who told me after my release that he needed what I taught him in my Adult Continuing Education (ACE) class. To Jason Lee, who sought my wisdom in becoming "a real man" while at FCI Edgefield. To Michael J. Thompson at FCI Edgefield who fought the ACCA defining burglary—and won. He thanked me for my Political Science class and his awakening as a result of it. I thank him for coming outside his box and taking the course. I need allies...

And to my mother, who surprised me and attended the farce of a trial in Chattanooga, Tennessee by the U.S. government, and to Barbara who walked with me through the fire.

I acknowledge Barbara Patterson, Gaye Evans, Michael Kaplan, Jim Gray and Vernola Buchanan who made sure that I wasn't alone. And to those many men who shared a cell with me and drank of the "fire and hope" that I had to offer about God, redemption and social and spiritual change while I awaited trial—and eventually, release.

Because of you, I made it here. Thank you.

Foreword

I am writing this foreword only two weeks before the 50th anniversary of the historic March on Washington for Jobs and Freedom. I was privileged to be one of the several hundred thousand participants, as a 19 year old college student. I still have the index card with my bus number from that day.

My parents met because they were both members of the Brooklyn Young Communist League in the late 1930s, so as a "red diaper baby" it was no accident that I was very fortunate to be have been taught to hate and fight against racism at every opportunity. Never be silent!

Perry Redd's book is an eloquent and passionate polemic in the anti-racist struggle, still ongoing and as necessary as ever. The murder of Trayvon Martin has reminded us once again that America is not yet at the stage where race has no relevance to the quality of life people of color experience. White supremacy continues its reign with a Black President, a paradox only if the relevance of class is not considered in its reproduction.

I retired a year ago as a faculty member of Howard University where I taught for 39 years. My courses focused on environmental issues and the history of life over geologic time, including the emergence of our own species some 100,000 years ago in Africa. If white Americans truly understood where their ancestors originated and why race has trivial biological standing the struggle to abolish white supremacy would be significantly empowered.

I enjoyed provoking my students with a simple question: "Who invented the white race?" Note that most of these students were African American. A few may have thought it was Yakub, the Black scientist in the theology of the Nation of Islam.

Historically, in 1676-77 the invention took place in colonial America as a consequence of the Bacon's rebellion of indentured laborers, a diverse population from Europe and Africa. Soon after, the legal system of racial oppression was created. "Interracial" marriage was outlawed. The brutal system of plantation slavery followed in the 18th and 19th century. As a construct with powerful and continuing social consequences, whiteness was invented to create a hierarchy essential for the ruling class to reproduce its economic and political power in capitalist U.S.A.

Theodore Allen's "The Invention of the White Race" is the seminal work that created the foundation for the scholarly study of the relevance of whiteness in our nation's political economy. The Irish became white, followed by Italians and Jews. I highly recommend Jeffrey Perry's recent article on the reissue of Theodore Allen's book, available at: http://www.zcommunications.org/theodore-w-allen-s-the-invention-of-the-white-race-by-jeffrey-b-perry.

However, as a mechanism of reproducing white supremacy, white skin privilege is a relative privilege, not absolute, except for the 0.1-1% class enjoying the towering heights of wealth and power. And even a minority of this class may renounce their absolute privilege if they look in the mirror and recognize their moral corruption. White supremacy isn't at root an individual problem, it is a systemic structural challenge in 21st Century Capitalist America.

Redd points out "In the United States, wealth is highly concentrated in relatively few hands. As of 2007, the top 1% of households (the upper class) owned 34.6% of all privately held wealth, and the next 19% (the managerial, professional, and small business stratum) had 50.5%, which means that just 20% of the people owned a remarkable 85%, leaving only 15% of the wealth for the bottom 80% (wage and salary workers). In terms of financial wealth (total net worth minus the value of one's home), the top 1% of households had an even greater share: 42.7%."

Harold Meyerson gives more recent data on income inequality and profit growth: "Between 2009 and 2011, the incomes of the wealthiest 1 percent of American families grew by 11.2 percent. Median household income has declined every year since 2008. Profits, meanwhile, have risen to their highest share of the nation's economy since World War II, while wages have sunk to their lowest share," citing Emmanuel Saez, University of California-Berkeley economist (Washington Post, August 7, 2013, A19).

Even more alarming news: 80 Percent of U.S. Adults Face Near-Poverty, Unemployment: Survey (http://www.huffingtonpost.com/2013/07/28/poverty-unemployment-rates_n_3666594.html).

And no surprise, African Americans have the highest poverty rate, with Hispanics close behind (latest data available, 2011): 27.6 percent of Black Americans, 25.3 percent of Hispanic Americans, 9.8 percent of white Americans (http://www.businessinsider.com/poverty-in-america-2012-9 - comments19). Redd further documents the disproportionate burden borne by African Americans for example, in school expulsions schools and drug arrests.

Of course, relative privileges have significant life-and-death consequences, even for white Americans who consciously reject racism, and this reality is brilliantly discussed by Perry Redd. Thus, it is above all the responsibility of white Americans who think they are opposed to racism to become part of a movement to abolish "whiteness" as a social construct, and destroy white supremacy forever.

The system of white supremacy must be recreated for each generation or the power of the 1% in society may be delegitimized to the point where we leave prehistory, the epoch of class exploitation, to the other U.S.A. that is possible, a huge step towards the other world that is possible, given U.S. imperial hegemony in the world system.

Turning to our hometown, Washington, DC, the intersection of race and class in our community bears careful study, as a guide to effective action. This intersection is critical to understanding the dynamics of District political economy. The "chocolate" city is becoming vanilla, though still mocha (African Americans still constitute about half of DC residents. The violations of human rights in the District are profoundly racist given the racial composition of the recipients of the most egregious effects of these violations, particularly children of color.

With Black Mayors and a long standing Black majority of the City Council in charge of our local elected government, this institutionalized racism is "an emperor with no clothes" outside the acceptable political discourse to the media opinion makers. Increasing polarization of rich and poor divides the community along both class and race lines. Hence probing into the dynamics of race and class is more relevant than ever.

Let's look closer at the economic and social status of our residents. DC has the highest income inequality in the nation compared to any state and virtually all cities, inequality which has progressively grown in the last 10-15 years, particularly from the inception of the Control Board regime. DC has among the highest child poverty and HIV/AIDs infection rates in the nation. Research demonstrates that income inequality in a community, state or nation is the fundamental driver of bad health.

A major contributing cause of these systematic violations of the human rights of our residents is the policy appropriately called "urban structural adjustment" coupled with the impact of Congress's neocolonial rule, similar to SAP applied by the World Bank/IMF to countries of the global South. This policy has included the erosion of democracy (e.g., our Mayor's change to school governance in the Home Rule Charter by Congressional action instead of referendum by District voters), tax cuts targeted to the wealthy, huge subsidies to the big corporate sector taken from our tax-derived revenue, gentrification, coupled with reduction of affordable housing and now closure of neighborhood public schools a component of a so-called school reform policy of privatization and attacks on unions.

I urge you to read the Report on State of Human Rights in DC available at **http://afsc.org/resource/report-state-human-rights-dc**. This report is an assessment of the human rights record of our local and federal governments since DC self-declared itself as a Human Rights City, on December 10, 2008, the first U.S. city to do so. Our District government and elected officials received Fs for Poverty reduction and income equality and Welfare of Children and D for Public Education. These grades were given in February 2012 and still stand as testimony to continuing human rights violations in DC for which our elected government bears a large share of responsibility.

But this is no time to retreat from political struggle. I was fortunate to participate in the historic Perry Redd City Council campaign this past spring, a major achievement in highlighting the human right violations of our Returning Citizens, the imperative need for a living wage for all workers in DC, and our long overdue struggle for self-determination, DC Statehood.

Our struggle for DC Statehood is both a civil and human rights campaign to expand U.S. democracy by ending neocolonial rule in the capital of our nation. The struggle for DC Statehood is of course a struggle for our political human rights, but also for the economic, social and environmental human rights of our residents and likewise the latter struggle empowers the struggle for statehood. This book will hopefully reenergize our human rights struggle, from our local community to the international arena.

David Schwartzman, Professor Emeritus, Howard University (dschwartzman@gmail.com)

Preface

Allow me to give thanks to ones who lit the fire in me...the fire for freedom. The ones who taught me sacrifice and exposed my willingness to give.

As a condition of your freedom, you must assess how much you're willing to give. If you give too much, then you've made your freedom ineffectual—unless you're a martyr. Freedom is not only a physical phenomenon, but freedom encompasses one's spirit, one's intellect and one's emotion. A prohibition on any one of those elements effectually holds one in bondage.

This text was written to inform Americans on where they've surrendered their actual freedom for an unreasonable facsimile. Simply because you can buy an X-Box or travel to the marina does not make you free. In America, you are not free to live wherever you choose. As of the writing of this book, if you are a gay American who wants to practice marriage to a same-sex partner, you can only get married and/or recognized as married in six states. Everywhere else, you are prohibited from practicing that freedom that other Americans might enjoy.

If you haven't guessed by now, I am not an intellectual, nor am I an academician. I likely never will be, though I need those who are to confirm what I live. I am an average working class American...who also happens to be Black. This is not a memoir of my "story," though facets of my story are within. I include those antidotes as confirmation of understanding and proof of my practical experience in my struggle for freedom.

In some areas of my hometown, though you own your home, you may not be able to cookout in your front yard. This is a decision made by people who don't pay your mortgage, nor employ you. Homeowners Associations are such an entity. Is that freedom? One must question his/her interpretation of freedom. In that, you must decide how much you are willing to give in order to obtain and maintain your ideal level freedom.

You hear the term "freedom" bantered about the politi-sphere, as if it really exists. We hear conservatives complain incessantly about President Obama taking their "freedoms," while crusading for policies that take others' freedom, like freedom to marry; even when George W. Bush had his eight years as chief executive, the assault on "freedom" raged fast and loose. But the reality is, there was nothing new about denial of freedom for Black Americans.

I want you free. I want my children free. You should too. This life in America should not be an eggshell walk. Being better off than Tunisia, Malaysia, Myanmar or Bolivia is only relative to not knowing true freedom within a societal context.

I was highly impressed with the historical context surrounding Nelson Mandela's leadership in Black South African's quest for freedom from apartheid. I also found it strange that white South Africans—and whites around the world—found that the South African system of apartheid was right and acceptable.

Just a little about Mandela: Nelson Rolihlahla Mandela was born in a village near Umtata in Transkei South Africa on July 18, 1918—in a mud hut (and it probably was really a mud hut, and not over-dramatized like most Americans attempt to make their heroes). His father was the Tribal Chief of Thembuland and after his father's death, the young Rolihlahla became the Paramount

Chief's ward to be groomed to assume high office. However, influenced by the cases that came before the Chief's court, he was determined to become a lawyer. After hearing the elders' stories of his ancestor's valor during the wars of resistance in defense of their fatherland, he dreamed also of making his own contribution to the freedom struggle of his people. That vision became my vision by the time I reached 30.

After receiving a primary education at a local mission school, Nelson Mandela was sent to Healdtown, a reputable Wesleyan secondary school where he caught on and assimilated well. After leaving school he then enrolled at an all-black college, the University College of Fort Hare for a Bachelor of Arts Degree where his leadership qualities began to shine. After being elected to the Student's Representative Council, Mandela started to live up to his Xhosa name **Rolihlahla**, meaning "stirring up trouble", and joined a student boycott which resulted in his suspension from the college.

Just that early segment of Mandela's life is enough to motivate one to be the change you want to see. At Mandela's passing from this life in December 2013, I embraced his struggle, stand and station by the end of his life. He chose to be free; he tried to free his people. The term freedom is not a light word to toss around. Most Americans cling to the concept. This is placed before us at a young age. Something inherently wells within us at the sense of the word. As children, we relish the idea by standing in the middle of an open space, spreading our hands and spinning around in circles. That's the most elementary form in which we can demonstrate what we mean by the word. Freedom gets major in every forum thereafter.

One of my close advisors challenged me to prove my point. Herein, I give you all of the reason in the world to get off the sideline and join with like-minded people to make the people in power do right, do you right or make those people in power yourself. Burn the barriers and get in the game!

As a condition of your freedom is designed to help you absolve yourself of the guilt that is placed upon people who demand justice—the right thing for the right reasons. Carrying the burden for being born into a system designed to fail and being required to run the race—without shoes while everyone else has them—is not your fault. I want you to walk away knowing why.

When you finally pass this book on to someone you care about, I want you to have released your mind from the colonialist submission that has been the "go along to get along" sub-consciousness you've lived with. I hope you would have seen that consumerism has not served your mind—or your life—well.

And lastly, I want you, my reader, to feel the urgency to act in some coherent fashion to change the current status quo. To desire the change from theirs to mine—for your own sake...and if not for you, then for the ones you love. Acting doesn't mean you have to do it alone. The internet has made it too easy for us to act in concert with others who also desire freedom. Go find them. My days on this earth aren't long. I may not see freedom, but that doesn't mean I don't want it for you. Whether Black, white or indifferent, as a condition of your freedom, I shall give you reason to act.

Chapter One

As A Condition of Your Freedom, You Cannot...
Ignore Racism

"We've got to face the fact that some people say you fight fire best with fire, but we say you put fire out best with water. We say you don't fight racism with racism. We're gonna fight racism with solidarity."
— Fred Hampton

If you are reading this book as a citizen of the United States, or one if its protectorates, then you are a victim of racism. Chances are you don't like that determination, but tough shit. It is what it is.

If you not "receiving" my proclamation, it's likely because you have 1) been fighting the bonds of oppression and refuse reality, 2) are a child of great privilege, or 3) tired of being labeled a victim. Of the three, I say "do you" on any, but the fact still remains that you are a *victim* of a sick and depraved social system.

America was built on the premise of racism. The hierarchal, male-dominated social structure that set the stage for all of the injustice, inequality and mayhem that this country has placed upon any people it has encountered, has poisoned you.

As much as you don't want to believe it, it is unnatural for men to enslave and/or oppress other men...but they do it anyway. Just look at Israel's treatment of Palestinians. Some attribute it to "sin nature," others to greed. Most do it because they can. Some say it's inherited, but whatever the scientific finding, it is what it is. I'm here to help you identify your role in this madness.

One of my favorite political analysts, author James Loewen describes it like this in *Lies My Teacher Told Me*[1]: "Perhaps the most persuasive theme in our history is the domination of black America by white America. Race is the sharpest and deepest division in American life. Issues of black-white relations propelled the Whig party to collapse, prompted the formation of the Republican Party, and caused the Democratic Party to label itself the "white man's party" for almost a century. Pretty simply, race is the foundation of this country's every problem.

I am a self-admitted "angry, black male." No, I don't rant and rave; I don't scowl and menace, though I have in my past and want to each waking day. It's not because that is my nature. It is because each day that I live (residing in America is immaterial), white males find yet another way to ruin the world and the lives of people within it. I am and have been an unwilling witness.

Whether it's the things they say, the propaganda they create, the positions they espouse or the acts they undertake, white males ruin other people's lives. Many do it unintentionally, while others do it with reckless abandon. Many use subtle and covert methods, while others play "The Sacrificial Lamb" role. No matter *how* it's done, it's done.

One of the most intimate elements of a man's character is his/her self-respect. The saying goes: "if a man doesn't respect himself, then how can anyone else respect him?" With that in mind, it's no wonder that a man gets highly offended when others step on his/her pride, dignity or identity. Yet, in America, there is an unwritten rule that a certain class of people can do that very thing to others with impunity...white males.

At every turn within our societal structure, within every set institution, white males exceed the boundaries that exist for all other Americans—including white women.

If there is a closed door, only a white male is expected to have the "authority" to not only open it, but enter. As for the rest of us, we stand idly by and act if that is fact.

I'm here to proclaim that the norm is no longer normal. That is a fallacy for times past. White males, both in my immediate surroundings, as well as the world stage have lost all credibility with me. Racism has been the vehicle for bringing me to this arrival point. I've been here for a while; I'm just waiting for others to get here...it's damned lonely though.

I cringe at the thought that, even today, white males are still teaching faulty logic and theory to their children. The idea of ethnic cleansing and Eugenics confirm for me that race is an evil concept and that it takes evil men to perpetuate those types of concepts. It also confirms for me that there are scared and fearful people walking the face of the earth. What I've come to learn is that unjustified fear leads to justified loathing.

Eugenics was (and is) an effort to breed "better" human beings by encouraging the reproduction of people with "good" genes and discouraging those with "bad" genes. Eugenicists effectively lobbied for social legislation to keep racial and ethnic groups separate, to restrict immigration from Asia, Africa and southern and eastern Europe, and to sterilize people considered "genetically unfit."

Elements of the American eugenics movement were models for the Nazis, whose radical adaptation of eugenics culminated in the Holocaust. We'd better be careful, because there are some working identifying racial differentiations as we breathe...don't sleep it.

The United States took Eugenics and ran with it, making it part of mainstream society. By 1928, 376 separate college courses, which enrolled 20,000 students focused on Eugenics. (Seldon) And an analysis of high school text books from 1914 to 1948 indicates that the majority presented Eugenics as legitimate. No wonder modern America was as racist as it was...or is. Takes a while for ugly to fade away.

As a society, we've grown past the curricularized legitimacy of Eugenics, but woven into the fabric of our social structure, we still possess the underlying belief in its use and legitimacy. Body type, survival, loneliness, ferocious lust and money are the only factors that may overcome our adherence to it. We still hold elements of its theory within us. That's why it is so hard to move beyond racism.

We are still mesmerized (at least white America is) with a royal marriage in England. These "royal" marriages are concerted efforts to keep "good" genes in the top echelon of the social structure. We stand in awe and applaud Eugenics today. How can we be so foolish? Even more to the point, how can Black people join in those festivities? These are blatant lessons on how to keep you (whoever you are) in or out the game. This is a type of commercial brainwashing.

A Tool of Racial Division

The growing narrative—that agitates me to the hilt—is how America has transcended the racial divide, and that all is okay now...well, it isn't.

Despite an enormous and persistent black-white wealth gap, the ascendant American narrative is one that proclaims our society has transcended the racial divide. But wealth is a paramount indicator of social well-being. Wealthier families are better positioned to afford elite education, access capital to start a business, finance expensive medical procedures, reside in higher-amenity neighborhoods, exert political influence through campaign contributions, purchase better legal representation, leave a bequest, and withstand financial hardship resulting from an emergency.

The wealth gap in the US is the most acute indicator of racial inequality. Since America is a capitalist country, wealth matters. Based on data from the 2002 Survey of Income and Program Participation, white median household net worth was about $90,000; in contrast it was only about $8,000 for the median Latino household and a mere $6,000 for the median black household. The median Latino or black household would have had to save nearly 100% of its income for at least *three consecutive years* to close the gap.

But more recently, Pew research analysis from 2009 revealed that the median wealth of white households is currently 20 times that of black households and 18 times that of Hispanic households.

These lopsided wealth ratios are the largest since the government began publishing such data a quarter century ago and roughly twice the size of the ratios that had prevailed between these three groups for the two decades prior to the Great Recession that ended in 2009.

The Pew Research analysis found that, in percentage terms, the bursting of the housing market bubble in 2006 and the recession that followed from late 2007 to mid-2009 took a far greater toll on the wealth of minorities than whites. That's why Barack Obama won the presidential election of 2008. From 2005 to 2009, inflation-adjusted median wealth fell by 66% among Hispanic households and 53% among black households, compared with just 16% among white households.

As a result of these declines, the typical black household had just $5,677 in wealth (assets minus debts) in 2009; the typical Hispanic household had $6,325 in wealth; and the typical white household had $113,149. That's pretty fair, huh?

Furthermore, 85% of black and Latino households had a net worth below the median white household. Regardless of age, household structure, education, occupation, or income, black households typically have less than a quarter of the wealth of otherwise comparable white households. It is an easy thing to perpetuate racism when you hold the preponderance of the resources.

In 1947, the median family—the one making more than half of all other families and less than half of all other families—made $23,400, according to the

Economic Policy Institute. Over the next three decades, median-income more than doubled, to $47,400 in 1977. In 2005, the median family made $58,400. (All these numbers are adjusted for inflation.)

Meanwhile, the incomes of earners at the 99.99th percentile of the income distribution—those making more than 9,999 out of every 10,000 other earners—have soared over the last three decades, from less than $2 million in the late 1970s to about $10 million in 2009. That's partially the reason for the groundswell of the Occupy Wall Street movement of 2011.

Since the election of Barack Obama, a growing belief has emerged that race is no longer a defining feature of one's life chances. But the extraordinary overlap between wealth and race makes a lie of the notion that America is now in a post-racial era. The smallest racial wealth gap exists for families in the third quartile of the income distribution where the typical black family has only 38% of the wealth of the typical white family. In the bottom income quartile—the group containing the working poor—a black family has a startlingly low 2% of the wealth of the typical white family.

Those who recognize the racial wealth gap but still embrace the idea of a post-racial America have crafted two explanations for this disparity. The first is that, in search of immediate gratification, blacks are less frugal when it comes to savings. Indeed, in an April 2011 lecture at Morehouse College, Federal Reserve Chair Ben Bernanke attributed the racial wealth gap to a lack of "financial literacy" on the part of blacks, particularly with respect to savings behavior. [2] This is the "blame the victim" methodology. The other reason is even more simplistic: they don't work hard enough. Do I even *have* to elaborate on that one?

One Bad Tactic Leads to Another

Allow me to interject another blatant instance socially-sanctioned American racism to further make my point. Here in my hometown of Washington, DC, we're currently undergoing an ugly era in the city's history: gentrification. The gentrifiers don't find it ugly, but would you if you were making out like bandits?

Whites have unashamedly taken the city over and used the economic sword to displace the greater majority black population. Nullified are the culture, history and respect for Blacks in targeted neighborhoods. Changes to Columbia Heights, U Street/Shaw corridor, H Street and Potomac Avenue came with grand disregard for the people who grew up in those now-gentrified neighborhoods. Bike lanes and outdoor cafes dot the city; the lifestyle of Europe has become DC's complexion.

With that change in demographics, comes the decline of the displaced. DC has always been racially segregated—if not legally, then practically. Schools are a good example. The achievement gap between black and white students in Washington is among the largest in the country, according to a 2011 federal study from the National Assessment of Educational Progress.[3]

Fourth-grade math scores were a prime example of the gap. Black students in D.C. scored an average of 212 points out of a possible 500; white students scored 262. That's a 50-point difference, which is twice the national average. The gap in New York City and Philadelphia schools is much smaller, somewhere in the range of 20 points. But a gap nonetheless...

Every two years, the U.S. Department of Education conducts the test, called "the Nation's Report Card." It is meant as a universal metric to compare school performance.

Now, you know that statistics like that bring about the neo-colonialist remedies of de-funding and closing public schools and blaming teachers. That's what happened in DC. The attacks on the schools became popular—at the expense of the Black community—with the gentrifiers leading the charge. What failed to get critical examination were the decades of under-funding and critical factors such as school suspensions.

No, really! Data suggest Blacks are two to five times more likely to be suspended or expelled than their white peers, and that the gap exists across the D.C. area's urban, suburban and rural school districts. The problems, which extend across the country, are among a host of concerns about school discipline being examined by the U.S. Justice and Education departments today. Yet we know that whites are intolerant to any behavior that isn't them. This is a snapshot the racism you cannot ignore.

An analysis by *The Washington Post* in December 2011 showed the phenomenon both in the suburbs of D.C. and in the city, from the far reaches of Southern

Maryland to the subdivisions of Fairfax, Prince George's and Montgomery counties.

Last year, for example, one in seven black students in St. Mary's County, Maryland were suspended from school, compared with one in 20 white students. In Alexandria (Virginia), black students were nearly six times as likely to be suspended as their white peers.

No one is allowed to challenge the "when" of those numbers, nor the "who" in them. Are the suspension occurring around standardized test dates, where if those "low-grade" students aren't in school during test times, then the "No Child Left Behind" scores are higher as to effect federal funding? The "who": is it white teachers with virtually no cultural understanding of Black boys quickly reporting unfamiliar behavior as "threatening," thus leading to unwarranted suspensions?

Never belaboring the issue of systemic racism, another instance comes to mind. The non-partisan group ProPublica compiled a report in 2011 that showed— through empirical data that White criminals seeking presidential pardons over the past decade have been nearly four times as likely to succeed in getting one as minorities.[4] Blacks have had the poorest chance of receiving the president's ultimate act of mercy (wouldn't you know it), according to an analysis of previously unreleased records and related data.

Now, don't get me wrong, this report wasn't a stunner, nor was it a revelation, but it was surprising that, not only did someone look into this, but that they didn't sugar coat their results.

These are instances that we all know, but cannot prove. Blacks rarely have the kind of access afforded to them—though that open records law exists—to confirm the thing we claim, so White Americans dismiss the claims of Blacks as mere paranoia—or worse, get accused of playing the race card.

The review of applications for pardons is conducted almost entirely in secret, with the government releasing scant information about those it rejects. We know the president's power to pardon is embedded within the Constitution. It is an act of forgiveness for a federal crime. It does not wipe away the conviction, but it does restore a person's full rights to vote, possess firearms and serve on federal juries. It allows individuals to obtain licensing and business permits and removes barriers to certain career opportunities and adoptions. I know because I research processes and parameters for applying for a presidential pardon while I was incarcerated at FCI Edgefield in 2009. I knew that I would have unreasonable barriers set before upon my release from federal incarceration. I was right.

Getting to brass tacks, from 2001 to 2008, President George W. Bush issued decisions in 1,918 pardon cases sent to him by the Justice Department, most involving nonviolent drug or financial crimes. He pardoned 189 people—all but 13 of whom were white. Seven pardons went to blacks, four to Hispanics, one to an Asian and one to a Native American. But that's just coincidence, huh?

To analyze pardons, ProPublica selected a random sample of nearly 500 cases decided by President Bush and spent a year tracking down the age, gender, race, crime, sentence and marital status of applicants from public records and interviews.

Now watch this: in multiple cases, white and black pardon applicants who committed similar offenses and had comparable post-conviction records experienced opposite outcomes.

Here's a case in point: a Black woman from Little Rock, fined $3,000 for underreporting her income in 1989, was denied a pardon; a white woman from the same city who faked multiple tax returns to collect more than $25,000 in refunds got one. You don't believe me? Go to the ProPublica report! In another case, a black, first-time drug offender -- a Vietnam veteran who got probation in South Carolina for possessing 1.1 grams of crack was turned down, while a white, fourth-time drug offender who did prison time for selling 1,050 grams of methamphetamine was pardoned. Now, the report didn't say what rationale the Justice Department used to come to their determination in either case, but for anyone who's not dead or on life support, we know why.

All of the drug offenders forgiven during the Bush administration at the pardon attorney's recommendation—34 of them—were white. Now if that isn't ironclad proof of institutional racism, then nothing is. One can deny, but has no leg to stand on.

Dismissive Tact

It is so easy for whites to dismiss *their* roles in the lack of American economic equality. It is also easy for whites to dismiss the benefits they've gained *from* American economic inequality. It is equally easy for them to discount the role of slavery's legacy that has predestined the imbalance of the scales today. That is the reason we cannot allow ourselves to be distracted, nor can we play the "race is no thing" game. It is a thing.

Just in mid-2011, NPR ran a story that did just that. NPR's Neda Ulaby reported on the "transformation" of the accusation of racism.[5] In a story on the phrase, "That's racist!" the anchor lead the story with the de-sensitizing slave: "Now, we dig into the meaning of a catchphrase that's become a staple in schoolyards and comedy routines: "That's racist." In the past, it was always a loaded challenge. It meant something to accuse someone of racism, but NPR posited, no more.

NEDA ULABY: "That's racist." It's practically a running bit on TV. Sometimes it doesn't even refer to race. Like in the show "Parks and Rec," in a scene about folding laundry.
(Soundbite of TV show "Parks and Recreation")

Mr. ADAM SCOTT (Actor): (as Ben Wyatt) OK, so you always separate your lights from your darks.
Ms. AUBREY PLAZA (Actor): (as April Ludgate) That's racist.
ULABY: Or in the sitcom "Community."
(Soundbite of TV show, "Community")
Mr. DONALD GLOVER (Actor): (as Troy Barnes) You're saying I could be a lawyer.
Mr. JOEL McHALE (Actor): (as Jeff Winger) I'm saying you're a football player. It's in your blood.
Mr. GLOVER: (as Troy Barnes) That's racist.
Mr. McHALE: (as Jeff Winger) Your soul.
Mr. GLOVER: (as Troy Barnes) That's racist.
Mr. McHALE: (as Jeff Winger) Your eyes?
Mr. GLOVER: (as Troy Barnes) That's gay.
Mr. McHALE: (as Jeff Winger) That's homophobic.
Mr. GLOVER: (as Troy Barnes) That's black.
Mr. McHALE: (as Jeff Winger) That's racist.

What I've learned is that whites have worked long and hard—since desegregation—to make racism go away, while still being what they're most comfortable being: racist.

Through mainstream media, sports and entertainment, America downplays the reality of inequalities enforced by these venues. What we know is that whites have a legacy of Constitutionally-imposed slavery and decades of Jim Crow at their backs. Just because legislation has been passed and signed into law that prohibits anyone in America from discriminating against someone else in America, doesn't mean those laws will be enforced. For forty-some years, whites have either created ways to bypass and undermine the law, pushed the limits to the outermost edge or disregarded the law altogether.

As a young man, I asked, "Why would someone *want* to be racist or practice racism?" It made no sense to me, until I joined the United States Army. I excelled at my studies into my military occupational specialty (MOS), yet as a Black soldier, I was despised by many of my white counterparts. I was from the north. My two immediate superiors were from Arkansas and Alabama, respectively. They failed not to remind me.

Beyond that was the fact that I was despised not because of my rank, status or work ethic, but for the color of my skin. They made efforts to remind me of that too. When I complained through the legal channels, I learned of the standards that had to be met. The offenders knew too, so they would do just enough to stay "off the radar." That's what whites do on racism's front lines while simultaneously whittling away at the legislative protections that are in place. When you are being degraded for issues beyond your control—like skin color—there shouldn't *have* to be benchmarks. You know what it is...and so do the perpetrators.

Thus, as in the NPR piece, whites use media to de-sensitize Americans to an obviously offensive practice. That's how media works: if you say something enough times, it becomes true. Remember that kids...of course that's insanity *unless you're the one under attack*.

As much as I hated this NPR piece, I'd like to think they were genuine in trying to expose how "crying wolf" on racist behavior, trivializes it:

ULABY: Rachels and his friends in Lexington, Virginia started saying "That's racist" about three years ago. And they do it, why?

Mr. RACHELS: I think I or other people just sort of do it as a way of mocking people, who are overly sensitive about race issues.

ULABY: Like the white kid who thought it was racist to say someone's black. Or - another story - the kid who asked if a schoolmate was Chinese. Another kid yelled, that's racist...

ULABY: "That's racist" works in comedy, Buress says, because it pushes buttons. Scholar Regina Bradley says it also works because racism's often expressed differently than from a generation or two ago.

Ms. BRADLEY: If it was the 1950s or when my grandparents were coming up in Jim Crow and somebody says that's racist, they're like, OK, well, duh.

ULABY: The segregated neighborhoods and swimming pools of Bradley's grandparents have yielded to more subtle forms of discrimination. That's reflected in how "that's racist" is being used - to shut down conversations or as a joke.

And not just in schoolyards or sitcoms. Glenn Beck used it as a cheap shot when he called the president racist a few years ago. [6]

Mr. GLENN BECK (TV Host): This guy is, I believe, a racist.

ULABY: Beck eventually apologized. Trivializing "that's racist" shows how much cultural confusion exists about race and racism right now, says Regina Bradley.

Ms. BRADLEY: I think it can acknowledge the problem and also sweep it under the rug at the same time.

ULABY: "That's racist" started as a virtual retort on Internet discussion boards. It was a little video clip from a cult TV show, an Black-American kid with the words "that's racist" underneath. People started dropping it into online arguments to quench or to inflame them.

Within the desensitizing nature of that story that NPR felt necessary to run, was the basis of racism: sadness, offense and minimization. Whites feel sad over the conversation, while blacks are the ones offended at the insult and whites aim to trivialize their need to insult someone else. Minimization breeds superiority; meaning, the one who minimalizes racism assumes the authority to judge who is "too sensitive" about it.

More to the point, the subtleties of de-sensitization are prevalent. Through fiction writing, whites can say what they truly want to say without taking responsibility for it. There is power in words. Courts know this; societies know this. For the Christian, by word, the world was formed. By the written word, laws are made, men are arrested and cultures are erased. Words are indeed relevant.

Change the Conversation?

There is a section of the country that advocates for "changing the conversation" from racial terms to human terms. On its face, that's admirable and utopian. Unfortunately, going that direction doesn't solve the problem, and cheats the victim.

There's a minority of the population who believes that speaking in economic terms will more readily unite us. They believe that all disparity can be addressed more effectively if we point out the economic imbalance in the country. Factually speaking, the economics of America was based upon the backs of racial superiority. It continues today.

Let us examine the Slave Trade Compromise[7] within the Constitution for an example. The story goes, northern free states were concerned that the economy developing was relying too much on slavery. Like drug addiction, they believed that if they relied on this system for too long they would never be able to get off it. To help the country get off the "slave economy," northern states proposed a ban on the importation of slavery.

Southern states were not willing to give up slavery so suddenly, because they believed their agriculture based economy (farming—with free labor) would not survive. Hell, they weren't going to do *that* labor.

The Compromise: The slave trade would continue for twenty years after the Constitution went into effect. Once the twenty years were up, the national government would be allowed to ban the importation of slaves into the United States. The bottom line is that economic disparity is rooted in the denial of one group of people access to the current economic empowerment tool: currency and wealth.

Unfortunately, money is green, not people. Economics is simply used as a veil to diminish the reality of racism.

Trials Are Not Justice

We watched yet another sordid episode of racial injustice during the span of the trial of George Zimmerman. Many who supported Zimmerman's acquittal referred to the trial as fair. This is yet another reason you cannot trust the oppressor.

The fatal shooting of the unarmed teenager Trayvon Martin by George Zimmerman took place on the night of February 26, 2012, in Sanford, Florida. Martin was a 17-year-old Black high school student. George Zimmerman, a 28-year-old multi-racial Hispanic American was the neighborhood watch coordinator for the gated community where Martin was temporarily staying and where the shooting took place.

The press only covered the trial because Blacks rose up and demanded that the police conduct standard operating procedures in investigation and charging.

Why should the people—Black people—have to demand that? Simply because the dominant class found it unnecessary to execute justice on behalf of a Black person in America.

The trial was a tainted affair. The local authorities weren't compelled to even arrest the shooter. Virtually all of the trial evidence was revealed to the public in the year prior to the trial. It appeared sabotaged from the beginning. Blacks were pessimistic about obtaining a just verdict as the verdict grew near.

Zimmerman was tried for second-degree murder and manslaughter and found not guilty at 11pmon Saturday, July 13, 2013. That's relevant because the verdict was announced at a time when most Americans are diverted from all things news. Then, I ask how a man follows another person in the dead of night and not expect to be confronted? The 17-year old Martin confronted this unknown pursuer. A teenager shouldn't be put in the position of a man.

Here's my analysis: Zimmerman felt that Black people should not be in *his* neighborhood, and more specifically, this young man was up to no good. This is what Professor Michelle Alexander termed "The Zimmerman Mindset."

You've got to ask why? Zimmerman admits that the boy committed no crime that he knew of, but his firearm emboldened him. He eventually realized he bit off more than he could chew and introduced a gun into a fist fight. Martin is dead. Dead men tell no tales.

Zimmerman changed his story and his evidence was tainted. More to my point, Blacks in America live in the hope that the system will bring forth it creed: justice for all. I am of the mind that it shall never happen during my lifetime. I've got a good twenty years left.

The system—in Florida—acquitted Zimmerman with a six-woman jury (lack of diversity); five of the six were white and somehow, some people expected justice? I wasn't one of those people.

Zimmerman wouldn't even have been charged had not the NAACP and other vehement activists hit the streets in Sanford. To this day, I ask whites how this could be just? The pro football star, Michael Vick, killed a *dog* and went to prison. He was Black. Just before the Zimmerman verdict, in the same state where Martin was killed, Marissa Anderson was sentenced to 20 years for firing a warning shot to fend off her husband when she felt threatened. Anderson was Black.

White Americans see the criminal justice system's adjudication in all of these cases as fair, as in, "they got a fair trial." Zimmerman isn't Black, thus he benefited from an oppressive and unequal system of justice, backed by a traditionally racist institution, the NRA.

George Zimmerman got to legally kill Trayvon Martin. State-sanctioned murder is a legacy in America. Just examine the era of lynching. Just because it's legal, doesn't mean it's right. Martin Luther King, Jr. reminded us: "Never forget that everything Hitler did in Germany was legal." Blacks must act up and act out to defend themselves as extinction looms. Don't allow white academicians to water down your exposure or racism as "hyper-sensitivity." Racial attack is real. You cannot trust the oppressor to protect your being.

Harmless to Whom?

The New York Post published the drawing, from famed cartoonist Sean Delonas, is rife with violent imagery and racial undertones in March of 2009

Racism is hidden behind satire. Know this, there's truth in jest. A chief means for putting forth the "Take Our .Country Back" agenda of the 2010 Tea Party surge was by the rhetoric of its representative talk radio commentators. The strategy worked, if only for a little while. Rush Limbaugh led the charge.

Whether it was playing the song "Barack, The Magic Negro" on his show or making light of "Obameo" [play on Oreo] cookies. It's so insane, it's funny; its so racist, that it isn't.

NPR contributes heavily to the minimalization of the scourge of racism. They use their few Black-themed programs as well as their regular Europeanized programming.

Michelle Martin's "Tell Me More" is a fine example. In January of 2012, Mrs. Martin aired "Stuff White Girls

Say: Funny of Offensive?"[8] featuring Franchesca Ramsey's viral video that received grand attention in the blogosphere. In the video, the white comedian dons a blonde wig and pokes fun at the silly, and sometimes offensive, things white girls say to black girls. Using comedy to talk about race is nothing new—and can be useful.

In this case, the insulting content of Ms. Ramsey's videos serves the useless purposes of whites in America. To minimalize offensive conduct—and excuse it as a joke—de-fangs the venom of racism and the calls to end it. This type of programming disempowers the advocates for racial respect, as well as racial equality. As a white person demanding the "right" to say nigger "because I can," is as insane as demanding to refer to disabled people as retarded. Don't do it. Furthermore, why would you **want** to say it?

From pictures of watermelons at the White House to police shooting monkeys, whites, once confronted, attribute their racism to "jokes." It's always funny when it's someone else. Just like slavery ("slaves enjoyed slavery") or segregation ("the Negro wanted his own water fountain"), the absurdity of someone taking joy in restriction or prohibition and being bound or someone being cool with inequality is too much to stomach.

These tools alone cannot stifle the quest for equality, for there is yet another tool that is fully necessary to complete the job of destruction of this truth: the Sambo. Sambo, being the historically derogatory term used to denote those Blacks who would do the bidding of the white oppressor. There is a grand need of the noteworthy Blacks to give this myth of no racism credence and credibility.

There have been attempts by apologists and racists alike that we, as a country, have become too "politically correct." That is a laughably insulting proposition. Who do *you* know is alright with being insulted for conditions they cannot control without cause? People with autism? Cancer survivors? Obese infants? Not everyone is a comedian, nor does everyone welcome insult and ridicule. Most work on themselves to minimalize that eventuality in life. Racists in America work diligently to break that line of humanity down to its lowest common denominator: free speech.

Not All Speech Needs to Be Free

No one wants to be censored. We're vain creatures who believe that what we have to say is always relevant and forever important. For that reason, most Americans cling to the First Amendment like a teenage crush. The problem is, we betray that love.

The First Amendment has been contorted to embrace racism and racist objectives. Speech is often used an effective tool to further racism and racially-based policies and ideals. This can prove extremely harmful. The Constitution was not designed to harm the population—any population—of the American citizenry. When that happens, a red flag ought to go off in your head that someone might have a valid concern rather than a hyper-sensitivity. If it's not necessary, then why say it?

Armstrong Williams, Shelby Steele, Herman Cain, Larry Elder, Dr. Ben Carson and Michael Steele are examples of the "Bojangling" black man needed to discount any and all claims that whites practice the same attitudes and principles of their American forefathers past. We give them credibility by patroning their opinions and musings. That's one of the pitfalls of capitalism. These people are harmful to the cause of positive societal change. This is the Booker T. Washington approach to addressing this social ill.

In 1895, Booker T. Washington gave what later came to be known as the Atlanta Compromise speech before the Cotton States and International Exposition in Atlanta. His address was then one of the most important and influential speeches in American history, guiding Black American resistance to white discrimination and establishing Washington as one of the leading black spokesmen in America. Washington's speech stressed accommodation rather than resistance to the racist order under which Southern Blacks lived. Whites embraced Washington's view because it was unthreatening to them and would "tame" Blacks into a submissive state.

Many have thought me to be uncompromising, thus I am accused of retarding the healing of racism. I respond that they are wrong. I cannot forgive my tormentors; I cannot forgive my oppressor—the white American male—*unless* he relents and repents. He won't do that.

Moreover, I cannot benignly live with the infliction of torment and oppression. Why, you may ask? Simply because, whites in America want to get straight to forgiveness, before atoning for the acts of hate, dismissiveness and degradation of an entire race of people (whether Black or Native American). Whites refuse to be accountable, and thus perpetuate the same behaviors that have caused centuries of mistrust.

This is the epitome of putting the cart before the horse. Healing cannot begin until both parties are certain of what they are healing from. All wrongs must be placed on the table, dialogued through to an agreed cause, effect and solution, then accepted by the majority population. Though many white Americans claim to be Christian, and hold fast to the belief that "America is a Christian nation" (which it isn't), they resist one of the most sacred tenets of Christianity: atonement.

Atonement is defined as reparation made for an injury or wrong. When confronted on that issue, white American Christians revert to the *Christian* definition (i.e., the *safe* one): reconciliation or an instance or reconciliation between God and humans. As long as they can keep reparation to an invisible being, they never have an obligation to deal with the visible one. That's why Christianity has lost credibility over the past 40 years—and thus, its membership.

More universally though, I'm still highly disappointed with the Blacks in America who have "made it." They feel neither connection nor obligation to aid in the fight to keep what they've got. They too often fail to recognize that the sacrifices made by others, got them what they've got. If not for freedom fighters, those opportunities would not have existed. The 1955 Montgomery Bus Boycott, the 1961 Freedom Riders and the 1963 Pettus Bridge martyrs are just a few instances of those who sacrificed to make the way for "them that got." More importantly, there are forces and factions seeking to take those gains away. Only numbers and working in concert can preserve those gains.

Racism is the root of American disparity and dysfunction. It has been the justification for lynching, imperialism and de-humanization. It is not only wrong, but unacceptable. As a condition of your freedom, you cannot ignore racism.

Chapter Two

As A Condition of Your Freedom, You Cannot...
Trust the Oppressor

Freedom is never voluntarily given by the oppressor; it must be demanded by the oppressed.
~Martin Luther King, Jr.

There are many truths that I have learned in my life. Among them, "people won't change until they're ready," "you can't make anyone do anything," and "a leopard can't change his spots." As funny as those sound coming out, they are indeed idioms of gold.

The resistance to change, I have found, is intertwined with the desire to maintain power and control...funny how that happens. Another thing I learned about men: they hate to lose. Whether the consequences are large or small, men don't like to lose, thus when one is on the brink of losing all bargaining chips, one will negotiate. We've seen this behavior with large corporations, political parties, captive prisoners or grand nations. It's a general characteristic of man. I said *general*. Not all men will...That's good news. You see, you don't have to go there. When things appear their bleakest, I implore you not to give in.

Negotiation should be a front end tool. America knows this well. We saw this personified when America was groping for a way to end its occupation of Afghanistan in 2011. After all of the talk, from Bush 43 to Obama: "we will not negotiate with terrorists," they went into talks with the Taliban and Afghan President (and puppet) Harmid Kharzi. Nevermind that the Taliban had been designated a terrorist organization since the 9/11 attacks.

What's the takeaway? The Taliban get it. There was no room for negotiation with an oppressor. Oppression is wrong...period. You've got to remember, the United States entered Afghanistan with grand intentions of making the Afghan population accept their medicine. When America began piling up uncomfortable casualties of war, they began to make promises. The Taliban wasn't going; promises mean nothing—ask the American Indian, ask the Palestinians, ask the Black man of American...you can't trust the oppressor.

It is strongly held principle, whether erroneously or not, that freedom is an unalienable right. Most white males hold true and dear to that concept—unless it's someone else's freedom we're talking about. What I know is that "no man embraces bondage."

How do we relate to one another?

There is a paradox that lies within the American experience...especially as a Black man. I have had fruitful and meaningful relationships with more than a few white males in my lifetime. Some have become mentors and have taught me lessons that have lasted throughout the duration of my adult life.

Unfortunately, the majority of my dealings have been what has solidified my deeply-held belief that they mean me no good. That the vast majority of white males want their social status to remain as it was 225 years ago.

I have had healthy male relationships with white men who, upon difficulty coming upon me (federal indictment, drug addiction, etc.) cut-and-run. Some of the very ones I thought were indeed "friends for life" turned out to be "friends for convenience." Two of the people who I saw as mentors, Bob Becker and Chris Woodhull, helped me identify my base instincts on community organizing, and we committed to healthy male bonds. Both men got elected to City Council in Knoxville, Tennessee. Yet, upon my indictment by federal authorities, their commitment to that male bond, quickly evaporated.

I always said that I understand, for their position on the Council was priority and that I didn't want to jeopardize their status. One never "feels" that, when he is in the midst of fighting the Goliath of the American judicial system. People in "high places" have a traditional purpose in our society: to aid you when you're in a tight spot. That rarely works for Black males.

More than anything, even after they each were term limited, they never returned to the table to sup with me. These occurrences only exemplified what I already believed: that white males only embrace Blacks when they 1) can make them money, 2) serve their needs, or 3) can entertain them. Heart issues are rare; a Huck Finn relationship is rare (not that I want one if those either!). And yes, Blacks emulate that character flaw too...

Back to the paradox, if one is spiritually grounded, then he/she knows that peace and a healthy communion with one's creator calls for living outside of one's self. The command given by Jesus to "love your enemies"[9] cannot go ignored. I battle constantly with, not only that command, but the internal reality to overcome my hurts and disappointments caused by years of intentional and unintentional afflictions at the hands of white America.

I think Dr. Martin Luther King, Jr. said something big when he advised:

> *"Now let me hasten to say that Jesus was very serious when he gave this command; he wasn't playing. He realized that it's hard to love your enemies. He realized that it's difficult to love those persons who seek to defeat you, those persons who say evil things about you. He realized that it was painfully hard, pressingly hard. But he wasn't playing. And we cannot dismiss this passage as just another example of Oriental hyperbole, just a sort of exaggeration to get over the point. This is a basic philosophy of all that we hear coming from the lips of our Master. Because Jesus wasn't playing; because he was serious. We have the Christian and moral responsibility to seek to discover the meaning of these words, and to discover how we can live out this command, and why we should live by this command."*

Dexter Avenue Baptist Church
Montgomery, Alabama
November 17, 1957

That position rests deep within me...but it doesn't rest well. It's like my soul sleeps with one eye open. I know that white America will do something else outrageous come the day after tomorrow. So I embody the internal spiritual struggle. I truly believe many men like me do the same. They just can't articulate it.

I honestly believe that many white men do too, yet for a different reason. You see, they know that their belief system is corrupt, contradictory and unjust. They know that they've been educated in an evil way, but it is now so deeply engrained within them, that they're powerless to turn back. What would their family and peers think of them? The accurate response to that is to look to the growing gay, white male population. You simply say, "The truth is what it is; I'm pretty much over it..."

But realistically speaking, white males aren't at that place—and that day won't come for at least another 40 years. I won't live long enough to see my prognostication come to pass. Why would anyone gladly relinquish their dominant status in a society? That's like expecting a heavyweight champion to give up his belt without a fight so that someone else may wear it...it just isn't happening.

We cannot allow white people to tell our story

I've come to learn that the most dictive, researched, eloquent of speakers cannot substitute for practical experience. I'm not speaking of history, per se, but the cultural peculiarities of people who are not them. There are intellectuals that have told the story of the disenfranchised with grand proficiency, but miss the passion of life.

For a Black male growing up in America, the works of the Howard Zinns, Douglas Blackmons, and James Loewens of the world have proven invaluable. They have also had publishing opportunities that Black story-tellers don't have. It's America. But moreover, they lack the credibility to accurately measure the impact and depth of centuries of racial and social injustice inflicted by white males.

There are qualified Black scholars and historians who lived with the descendants of and victims of institutionalized injustice. There are those like the DC-based historian of the Black-American diaspora, C.R. Gibbs who is ancestrally connected and has immersed himself in the struggle and lives of Blacks in America, but of course, are ignored when it comes to credibly telling the story of the under-class.

This is a snapshot of institutional oppression. An unknown quote says "The best way to change history is to become a historian." No, I'm not saying that Zinn or Douglas or Loewen would ever change history (I treasure their research and writings), but the vast majority of my community of people have never heard or, much less read, their writings. This is chiefly because oppressed people don't trust them. And the history of this country gives them cause.

Overall, It is unacceptable for Native Indians, Black and oppressed people overall to allow others to tell our stories. It always comes up short on facts, and leaves our progeny forever weakened. That's what an oppressing class wants.

We're not having picnics

My life partner was organizing a gathering of fellow Washingtonians for a social reunion of natives of the District. On a Facebook thread, they collectively choose to hold an outdoor event. Most wanted to have a picnic.

Subsequently, a young man named Pedro informed the thread of the origin of the word "picnic" and it's evolution within the Black American—essentially having a most negative connotation. Many on the thread were grateful for the education that Pedro offered, for some had no idea. But then, there were others.

Those others were offended at the history lesson and commenced to attacking Pedro on the thread. "It's unfortunate that you've reached into your personal dictionary" said one of the resistors of the information. One said, "The title of the event has already been chosen; we're not changing it!" The insults were hurled on-line.

As a result, people started searching for themselves. They found that the origin of the word is medieval French and according to some sources, the story is "urban legend." The resistors took the urban legend posts and used those as confirmation of their positions, disingenuously standing firm to retain the label picnic. Their position was further shored with the premise that "we've always done it that way." I was floored at the culmination of events around the organizing. Several of the resistors quit the project because their comfort zone was challenged.

I'm of the mind that past traditions will keep us enslaved. Just because that's the way it's been done, doesn't mean we have to keep doing it that way.

Whether picnic or nigger, someone used the term as a means to attack Black people. It's use was institutionalized to demean Black people, so why would we perpetuate this harmful language weapon?

Several of the resistors, in their condescension and dismissive attitudes toward Pedro, began to quote the Bible (funny how Christianity comes into to play). I would contend that Jesus even said that we shouldn't follow the traditions of men. I didn't want this book to be a pep rally for religion, but I will specifically quote the man:

Well hath Isaiah prophesied of you hypocrites, as it is written, This people honoreth me with their lips, but their heart is far from me. Howbeit in vain do they worship me, teaching for doctrines the commandments of men. For laying aside the commandment of God, ye hold the tradition of men, as the washing of pots and cups: and any other such like things ye do. And he said unto them, Full well ye reject the commandment of God, that ye may keep your own tradition.

The term "colored" was at one time acceptable language in reference to the formerly enslaved African descendants in America. Through dogged self-determination and the insistence of self-identity, those citizens re-defined the terms. The term "Colored"[10] was no longer acceptable and thus, rendered obsolete.

Just because that's how we've done it, doesn't make it the right thing to do. We saw this evolution with the term "Negro", "boy" and "nigger". Three terms that found re-definition in our country.

My point again is, just because that's how we've done it, doesn't make it the right thing to do. I hold fast to the premise that we progress in this country and this society. Yes, there are those who want to "take our country back," but they always fall on the wrong side of history. We witnessed a resistance to this in the election of 2012.

It's unfortunate that many of us get stuck on what we know, instead of walking into what we don't know—the epitome of ignorance. What we observe is that those "traditionalist" are often found in positions of authority. They maintain that authority by regurgitating the old adages and attitudes with dogged non-compromise. They can reach into your past—your psyche—and peak your comfort zone with the familiar beliefs of those who taught you, thus, cementing their credibility *with you*. They end up on committees, as lead organizers and even elected officials. Many perpetuate the status quo.

In this case, since the resistors couldn't use picnic, they quit. This is what "no compromise" looks like. We see this in today's Republican party—holding on to the traditions of their fathers (who were, incidentally, colonists, slaveholders, racists and Euro-white supremacists).

This is harmful to the American progressive ideal. Patriotism, pursuit of happiness, liberty, family values are "*Redd flag*" terms that evoke those traditions of their fathers...that traditionalists want to "take our country back" **to**. Whether urban legend or actual fact, Blacks cannot fall prey to the *picnic mentality*. The traditions of our [Black] fathers were overwhelmingly mindsets of submissiveness, docility and fear, regarding our relationship with white America. Nothing is absolute; there were those who resisted the status quo, some in the best way they knew how: self-deprecation, slothfulness, self-destruction, cunning, escape, or even suicide.

Those that enjoy the benefits that oppress others, shall always find it hard to let go. As with Palestine, Israel doesn't want them recognized as a nation state; it wouldn't benefit them. Israel will call for peace, but practice oppression. What do you expect Palestine to do? As a condition of your freedom, you cannot trust the oppressor.

Chapter Three

As A Condition of Your Freedom, You Cannot...
Rest Easy

"The arrogance of success is to think that what we did yesterday is good enough for tomorrow."
— William Pollard

If you think the war is over, watch for unseen land mines. The adversary won't rest until you are annihilated. That's the nature of man.

I herein appeal to man's greater nature. Co-existence within a societal structure calls for self-control; a reigning in of the carnality and brutality of our lowest capabilities. In other words, we don't have to be what we don't want to be.

For all of those positing the theory that the era of racism is over, I emphatically argue that this position is a fallacy...period. Just recently, I listened to a June 2011 airing of the Diane Rehm Show, NPR radio program with BBC's Katty Kay as the guest host. They floated to the public the justification of genetic testing to determine potential criminality in individuals.[11] You know that Blacks were the targets, right?

This was the opportunity to de-sensitize the general population to past stereotypes that blacks are more predestined to commit criminal acts. This, while the Casey Anthony trial was underway, Natalee Holloway had still not been recovered and the capture of Whitey

Bulger was at the head of the news. It affirmed for me that white people are indeed crazy.

John Laub, director of the National Institute of Justice, Benson George Cooke, president of the Association of Black Psychologists and John Paul Wright from the University of Cincinnati School of Criminal Justice were the panelists (for disclosure's sake, I interviewed Dr. Cooke on my radio show shortly after this show aired).

One of the panelists, Dr. Cooke, argued my position that hit the nail on the head, that criminal behavior is a byproduct of societal conditions. For example, rich people commit less crime solely because they possess more assets and money gives one access to more resources. Race is a misnomer.

The fact is that there are four chief reasons for criminal acting:
- Jobs
- The state of the economy
- Opportunity
- Prosecution and sentencing

It's impossible to live a "normal" American life because here are those who are perpetually fearful of losing their higher status in this American society. Fear, unfortunately breeds an uneasiness within and is translated onto other demographic groups. I'm specifically speaking of white Americans, as a whole, live in fear and support those that do also.

Dr. Benson Cooke, Ed. D.
The Association of Black Psychologists

The Israeli Jews are concerned about defending Israel from Palestinian assaults when they have all the nuclear weapons. We saw this overkill in rhetoric and action in November of 2012 when Israel bombed Gaza—and killed 139 Palestinians—for what it called retaliation for Hamas firing rockets into Israel territory (five Israelis were killed).This is a non-sensible proposition. They know it, but because they possess the resources and support of Western European nations—with resources—they continue to beat the drum of unjustified fear. The victors are those who control the message...in this case, Western nations.

As organizers of a flotilla seeking to challenge Israel's naval blockade of the Gaza Strip prepared to embark on their voyage in 2010, Israeli officials mounted an increasingly vocal campaign to discredit the activists, depicting them as planning violence against troops preparing to intercept the ships. Their aims were to bring food aid and supplies to the [darker-skinned] Palestinian Arabs residing in Gaza.

The effort reflects a high level of concern among Israeli officials about the potential impact of the maritime protest. Israeli commandos who boarded a Turkish ship in a similar flotilla in 2010 reportedly encountered resistance and killed nine people, provoking international condemnation that forced Israel to ease its land blockade of Gaza. Israel didn't apologize...and never will, though they never found caches of weapons they accused that flotilla of shipping to Gaza.

History reflects that Israeli newspapers were filled with reports from unnamed military officials, charging that sacks of chemicals, including sulfur, had been loaded onto flotilla vessels with the aim of using the materials against Israeli soldiers. The reports, cited military intelligence sources, said that some activists had spoken in preparatory meetings of their desire to "shed the blood" of soldiers and had threatened to kill those who might board their ships.

Israelis, of course, never revealed (and never will) the source of their accusations. Though wrong, the vast majority of white Americans, still supported Israel. The U.S. Secretary of State, Hilary Clinton, unapologetically supported this disinformation campaign...all based in fear. "Coming to kill," said a headline in the Maariv newspaper over a photo of one vessel.[12]

This principle of disinformation to foment fear is often supported and given credibility by "scientific" research. Back to the June 2011 Diane Rehm Show...Dr. Benson Cooke posited three determinate factors that skew "credible" findings.

One, who is doing the research? "The reality is we're still using a scientific approach that, if you don't have people sitting at the table who represent a diverse worldview or a diverse cultural sensitivity and degree of competence, then you're going to run into some problems with what the outcome is going to be," he said. That speaks to my point earlier: the victors are those who control the message. They will **never** look like criminals—according to _their_ findings.

Dr. Cooke's second point was, what the experimental design is going to be? "In many instances, if we're looking at whom the control group is—for example, that would be the norm. [So what's] the norm based upon versus what the control experimental group—this is the one that deviates from the norm. You're probably going to get deficit modeling. In that context, research that's been done using European Americans or whites as the norm, basically results in Black-Americans looking pathological."

And then, Dr. Cooke makes the third point that "when we're talking about crime, what kind of crime? For example, if you're looking at some of the work that's been done by Michelle Alexander in her book, *The New Jim Crow*,[13] she highlights that fact that in many instances you have individuals who, if they're using, for example, powder cocaine, faced a lower sentence of time versus those who are using crack. Same product [chemically and scientifically], but, socially and legally, there is this difference." Which solidifies my often-made point: the victors are those who control the message.

Fear is a hell of a motivator. In mid-September of 2011, Republicans scored an upset victory in a House race that started as a contest to replace Rep. Anthony Weiner after he resigned in a sexting scandal but became framed as a "referendum on President Barack Obama's economic policies."

For racists in America who loathed the idea of a Black man leading the country and serving as the face of the United States, his policies were used consistently as the cover for their racism. Nothing he could do—*even for them*—was good enough.

Retired media executive and political novice Bob Turner defeated Democratic state Assemblyman David Weprin in the 9th District of New York's special election to fill the seat vacated by Weiner, the seven-term Democrat who resigned in June of that year. Turner had around 54 percent of the vote to Weprin's 46 percent in unofficial results. The race was supposed to be an easy win for Democrats, who have a 3-1 ratio registration advantage in the district.

Weprin, a 56-year-old Orthodox Jew and member of a prominent Queens political family, seemed a good fit for the largely white, working-class district, which is nearly 40 percent Jewish. That "jewishness" is where the fear card got played.

Even though Obama had bent over backward on all substantive issues concerning Jews, Turner spouted Obama's disdain for the Israeli state. It made me sick! Despite being a heavily Democratic district, Israel became one of the biggest issues in the race for Jewish voters who were reportedly upset at President Obama's call to return to Israel's pre-1967 borders.

Given that Obama upset Blacks, Middle Eastern allies, human rights activists, environmental activists, anti-war activists and the world by standing by Israel when they refused to stop building settlements in the West Bank, didn't demand Israel apologize for killing American citizens while blockading a humanitarian aid flotilla to Gaza or even vowing to block the Palestinian's effort to request state recognition from the United Nations.

All positions that fall diametrically oppositional to the so-called liberalism of Obama, wasn't even on the radar when Turner stoked the fear of these white, New York Jews. Fear was undergirded by race.

There's a quote by Stokely Carmichael that I use in the introduction to my song, "Militantt": "In this country, you were to think that white people were gods...that they had the *right* to give *us* our freedom!" When I think on that alone, I know that there will be people I cannot trust...in particular, ones who oppress—whether he/she means well or not.

Martin Luther King, Jr. said, "Freedom is never voluntarily given by the oppressor; it must be demanded by the oppressed." We cannot trust that someone else has an altruistic bone that itches today; we must only trust in what *we* are willing to do about our circumstance. It is not our fault we are oppressed, discriminated against, lied to or deceived. That's *their* issue. It is our fault when we have done nothing about it. Since when do you think you can stop the devil from being devilish?

In mid-July of 2011, the suspect in the deadliest attack in Norway since World War II carried out an Oklahoma City-type mass shooting and bombing, and the perpetrator claimed to have worked with two other cells. Anders Behring Breivik, acknowledged carrying out the attacks, but said the attacks were necessary to prevent the "colonization" of the country by Muslims. He accused the Labour Party of Norway, whose members were targets of the mass shooting, of "treason" for promoting multiculturalism.

Breivik killed eight people on July 22, 2011 by setting off a car bomb in downtown Oslo that targeted government buildings, then traveled 20 miles to Utoya Island and shot and killed 68 teens and young adults in an ambush at a political youth retreat. Never mind he methodically shot and killed children in his process, he saw fit to correct a racial "problem" within his world. Sadly enough, he's not alone.

There are many individuals—who coalesce into groups—who find it necessary to cleanse a sovereign nation of its "dirty people"—i.e., people of color. The ones who perpetuate this "purification" are generally white males. People in the Arab world may also hold this idealism of "cleansing." And as such, we cannot rest easy. Racism, exclusivity, classism, homophobia, sexism or elitism shall never die. You cannot believe that it will.

I always teach young men that they come to place of consciousness around 33. This Breivik guy, was 32 years old. Breivik was a suspected right-wing Christian extremist who appeared to have written a 1,500-page manifesto ranting against Muslims and laying out meticulous plans to prepare for the attacks. He told investigators during interviews that he belonged to an international order, The Knights Templar, according to Norwegian newspaper VG, which cited unnamed sources. Maybe he did, or maybe in his own mind, but whatever the case, white superiority and preservation (fear) is the basis of this belief system.

He described the organization as an armed Christian order, fighting to rid the West of Islamic suppression. He also told investigators he had been in contact with like-minded individuals and said he counts himself as a representative of this order. He was likely crazy as a bat in the belfry, but unfortunately, crazy didn't stop his incessant desire to "cleanse" his country. He reportedly wanted to "take his country back." Does that sound familiar?

Let us be reminded of the Troy Davis saga, the Georgia death row inmate who was executed— murdered—in September 2011. High-profile figures, including former President Jimmy Carter, said there was too much doubt surrounding Davis' conviction and that his execution called the entire death penalty system into question.

Activists organized, called and marched. We thought we had made significant headway in calling into question the reasonable doubt of his guilt. Many of us thought that we had won a stay of execution when, at 7pm, the scheduled time of his execution by lethal injection, the Supreme Court purportedly stepped in to review the case.

Cheers went up around the nation in belief that a stay was imminent. The night drew on until 10:30 or so, they announced that Davis would be dead within the half hour...and he was.

When you think you've made some headway, they pull the rug from under you. You can't sleep; you can't rest, because they're coming all the time.

You may recall the U.S. mid-term elections of 2010. The theme of Tea Party supporters was to "take our country back." Though subdued, the mission is the same: to take their country back. What's fallacious about that concept is that the country is not "theirs." Through the evolution of time, labor and lives, the country belongs to a conglomerate of people. But you can't convince them of that fact.

Or, the election of 2012, where conservative Republican activists pushed legislation to enact voter I.D. laws, which subsequently disenfranchised Black, poor and other people of color disproportionately. Seeing that they would lose elections nationwide simply on the divisiveness of their social policies, conservatives had 30 states enacted that would in the words of Pennsylvania House Majority Leader, Mike Turzai call "Voter I.D....done!"

Unfortunately, the 2013 session of the Supreme Court made Turzai's proclamation real. The Court ruled that Section 4 of the Voting Rights Act, which determines what states and jurisdictions are covered by Section 5, is invalid after less than 50 years of protecting African Americans and people of color. The currently covered areas are places that historically have disenfranchised people of color, or those for whom English is their second language. Southern states that previously discriminated against potential Black voters had to pre-clear their changes of law with the Justice Department prior to enacting the change. No more...

Oh, back to "take our country back," I've even had people—pro and con—ask me, "back to what?" Though I find that senseless to ask, I answer: back to the days when all that was wrong, was normal. All of the erroneous value systems we've inherited from slavery was and is considered appropriate—even natural.

James Loewen—a white male—in *Lies* says it like this: [the idea] of whites to be on top, blacks on the bottom. In its core our culture tells us, including African Americans—that Europe's domination of the world came about because Europeans were smarter. In their core, many whites and some people of color believe this. White supremacy is not only a residue of slavery, to be sure. Developments in American history since slavery ended have maintained it.

What I know is that on the micro level, we cannot rest easy. It is easy to rest in one's idyllic hopes for America. I did in my teen years, but was quickly proven wrong as I entered adulthood. This brings me to the story of Tyra Batts of Buffalo, New York in fall of 2011.

I believe we're rapidly digressing from the progress we had achieved through the blood and sacrifice of our enslaved forbearers and civil rights warriors. I expounded upon how we can't take an inch of our progress for granted in a *Socially Speaking* commentary.

A Buffalo girls basketball team was suspended after the players allegedly used a racial slur as part of their pre-game cheer. If it was enough to get someone suspended, then you *know* what the slur was...

Tyra Batts, the sole Black-American on the Kenmore East High School's squad, told the Buffalo News that her teammates would hold hands before the game, say a prayer and then shout "One, two, three (nigger!)."[14] Now, I have to ask you why anyone—Black or white—would do that, but you know what it is. It's really simple: White people do it because they can!

The behavior came to light when Ms. Batts was suspended for getting into a fight about the use of racial slurs during practice, according to the newspaper. Now, I know me; I would've been in fistfights over this too—even at my age.

I was kicked out of the military in the early 1980's for that same thing. It retarded the trajectory of the rest of my life. As I aged, I realized, I could've done some things differently. Though, at the time, I went through the prescribed channels to address racial threats and discrimination.

Unfortunately in my case, the system was ill-responsive; even blaming the victim. After I saw that the "authorities" would do nothing to intervene, I took direct action...and busted some heads!

Ms. Batts said that she was alarmed by the cheer, but had been outnumbered and told that the use of the slur was just a team tradition. "I said, 'You're not allowed to say that word because I don't like that word,'" she told the newspaper. "They said, 'You know we're not racist, Tyra. It's just a word, not a label.' I was outnumbered." This scenario is not a surprising one. You see, whites echo the very excuses we, as Black Americans, make when this vile language comes out: it's just a word.

The N-Word has never gone away and it's more than "just a word." It was used during the country's infancy as a demeaning and degradation tool toward the enslaved imported Africans. Don't be fooled, words have power. "I love you" has spawned many a baby. "The sentence of death" quote has killed many a men. Words have power. Even Christians believe that God *spoke* this world into existence. Now **that's** power!

This incident is more than unfortunate...it is indicative of what we—Black Americans—allow. We haven't excused it from the English language. Until **we** make it unacceptable, white America won't find it unacceptable. I watched my first Paul Mooney performance the other night, and the comedian's liberality with the word does us no favors and great harm. He's a one comedian I'd never heard of before a Bush-era video was brought to my attention. He is a socio-political conscious individual, and liberally used the word "nigger" in all references.

He has the right to say what he so chooses, but the irreparable harm cannot be calculated. Though we relish freedom of speech in America, all speech doesn't **need** to be free. Though some feel that language is of no consequence, all dynamics of race (voting, health care, criminal justice, etc.) are relevant, important and significant, and thus need to be on the table.

Incidentally, the 15-year-old eventually exploded after a practice when a teammate called her a 'black piece of (expletive).' She says she got into a fight with the girl later in school. I know what the child was feeling, especially when you're supposed to be part of the "team." I was 18-years old and under the belief that in the army, we were all green. How wrong I was.

"It was a buildup of anger and frustration at being singled out of the whole team," Ms. Batts told the newspaper. Her suspension was shortened after the principal learned of the racial allegations. At least a dozen girls were suspended. Incidentally, Ms. Batts initially received a longer suspension than any of the white girls. How ironic, right?

Some of the team's former players who took to Twitter seemed to have little knowledge of any "tradition" the team had of racial chants. Collusion and cohesion was the same tactic used when I filed my complaint of racism while I was stationed at Fort Campbell, Kentucky. I was the sole Black Canon Fire Direction Specialist in my unit. They knew it. They, my tormentors and those up the chain of command, worked in concert to diminish my claims. Of course, the focus turned to my "attitude."

"You (racist) b—-," a 2010 graduate tweeted. "Glad I'm out of there." Another one added, "Haha oh yeah that Ken East crap that's going on. I want no part in that." Honestly, who does? When it's all over said and done, children or adults, racism in America is alive and well. Our children are victims—Black and white. The perpetuation of this poison has retarded any progress that this country has seen. That's the objective for those who in positions of privilege.

So in the final analysis, I reiterate: you cannot rest easy. You as the underclass, the minority, have to stay on-guard and aware that you are constantly under attack. You are under attack for things you do not control. You don't have to be decimated though. You can battle the assault without becoming like your assailant.

Organizing, education and participation in the political process are the necessary tools for sure victory in this

American war. But unfortunately, with every win, there's a new battle. They don't quit. You can't rest easy because the Timothy McVeighs of the world never die.

Chapter Four

As A Condition of Your Freedom, You Cannot...
Compromise Your Principles

"It's easy to make a buck. It's a lot tougher to make a difference."

~Tom Brokaw

America is a country of vast contradictions. It often holds fast to the concept of principle; of a maintaining a moral compass. The insistence of right versus wrong stands high within American socialization. Everyone is expected to have principles and adhere to them.

A common refrain circulating throughout the nation's urban centers is the quiet voice of Americans asking the Rodney King question: "can't we just all get along?" Some think we place too much emphasis on race. What I know is that Black people in America don't *want* to focus on race. Unfortunately, they are consistently forced to confront the 800-pound gorilla in the room, race.

The challenge in that reality is that Blacks have fought to face racism on its own terms, which is too often not the case with the mainstream of America. Here is a fact: Blacks in America have always wanted to "just get along." Because of the fears of whites in this country, Blacks have not been able to follow "The American Dream" to its completion.

In this present day, we have a cloud of fear and
loathing hanging above our heads in the form of Tea
Party politics. The era of "Take Our Country Back"
during the 2010 political season is yet another reason
why we can't "just get along." Many in that mindset
pursued the ideology of "going back to the
Constitution." This, of course, for Black people, is
unacceptable. What's funny is, white Americans know
it's unacceptable.

During the 2012 presidential campaign, as a Tea
Party-backed candidate, Minnesota Rep. Michelle
Bachmann evoked the real vision of those who longed
for that day. It wasn't so much going back to the days
of the Founders, but more so, going back to the
days—and actions—of Wilmington 1898.

A quick history lesson: The Wilmington Insurrection of
1898, also known as the Wilmington Massacre of 1898
or the Wilmington Race Riot of 1898, occurred in
Wilmington, North Carolina on November 10, 1898
and following days; it is considered a turning point in
North Carolina politics following Reconstruction.

Originally, it was labeled a "race riot" (the winner
defines the terms). I think "riot" is often wrongly
defined. It wasn't a riot, whites know what they
wanted, and Blacks intended to protect themselves.
You see, a riot has no intended direction or objective.
It is now also termed a *coup d'etat*, as insurrectionists
displaced the elected local government—comprised of
a majority of Blacks.

This event is the only instance of a municipal
government's being overthrown in US history.
Basically, it was treason. This is the dream of the Tea
Party, the Minutemen and those within the John Birch

Society. (During the fall of 1874, however, after a contested gubernatorial election, thousands of insurrectionist militia of the Democrat John McEnery fought the Battle of Liberty Place, displaced the elected state government based in New Orleans, and occupied government buildings for a few days before retreating when federal forces showed up.)

In the Wilmington Insurrection, Democratic white supremacists illegally seized power from an elected government, running officials out of the city, and killing many blacks in widespread attacks. Among their weapons, they used a Gatling gun mounted on a wagon. Why do you think white males are so avid in their support for gun rights and the National Rifle Association?

These people took photographs of each other during the events (good thing there was no Facebook!). Although residents appealed for help to Governor Daniel Lindsay Russell and President William McKinley, they did nothing in response. That's what Tea Partiers want today. That's why they wanted Obama to be a one-term president. That's why they want "government out of our business." It's crazy, unfathomable and selfish, but it what they wanted. The objective of this constituency is to mute the power of the President. That's what the Glenn Becks were for...

What's worse is that these neo-conservative-minded people will tell you that their beliefs are based in principle. Not only that, but that their principles are right. If you say anything enough, you'll believe it.

I came to a point in my life, around 33, where I began to ask, "Why is there such a different mindset that desires my demise?" I saw factions seeking to eliminate Affirmative Action in my teens, while my mother was in college. Even at that age, I could see that black people were on the short end of the educated class and wealth scale. I was also clued in that the two went hand-in-hand.

At 33, I began to wonder about the mountains my child would have one day face if things continued to deteriorate. I saw the attacks on welfare and the stereotyping of the welfare mother. I knew that the picture drawn was inaccurate—at least as far as the families in my neighborhood. I realized in the early 80's that there were forces after my soul...or at least my existence.

Those forces held up the banner of principle. I guess principle is defined as a fundamental truth or proposition that serves as the foundation for a system of belief or behavior or for a chain of reasoning. These people—white Americans—had a belief system (B.S.) that called for my (Black Americans) demise. I was walked into that truth. There were three fundamental beliefs: that we should serve them, that white women were the standard of beauty and that black men were more often than not, bad guys. Those three things stood out for me at an early age. White people I encountered were fine with that. It appeared that Blacks were too. Except my mother...

My mother, Jackie, was persistent in teaching me that none of those three things were factual, nor acceptable. She was clear to point out America's sordid past and that the society was set up in a servant-served structure; but we didn't have to fall into it. She taught me that "Black is beautiful"— especially Black women! I caught on to that one early. She emphasized that Black men were great.

Even among the pathetic stories that pervaded our environment, the Black male had persevered through some of the most despicable and unspeakable acts in human history.

During my youth, I was taught a fundamental truth. That whites have the upper hand in this society into which I was born, but it didn't have to remain that way. It was neither right nor earned. This condition was the result of years of injustice and contortion. I learned that the principle that America placed before me, was defined by the very people who sought to stunt my growth—and eventually would seek my soul.

Perverted, twisted perception of principles

Most of us have been indoctrinated with what it means to be American. That's not necessarily a bad thing. The ideals and concept that a nationalist ethos that purports to adhere to principles of "life, liberty and the pursuit of happiness" is an honorable objective. Unfortunately, as we grow in this society, we learn that this labeling is a propaganda tool to garner submission.

When I came to the knowledge of the history of the American Indian/Native American, I entered an era of soul searching. Even with the teaching of African slavery in America, I wasn't as inquisitive as to the validity of American principles. I knew we were "overcoming." But what was stolen from us—Black people in America—wasn't tangible. I couldn't see it; but the accounts of swindling and outright taking of lands that Americans hold dear today brought me into another place: Manhattan, Georgia, Florida...the Trail of Tears.

The fact that most of my childhood teaching, the conquest of the American Indian was left out of the curriculum. Public schools were forbidden from dispensing that story. I was taught about "Manifest Destiny," or at least the "sea to shining sea" part. That brave pioneers forged this country that we all can enjoy and call home. Early on, I wasn't taught that it was by theft, a principle left out of the American Way.

This was when I began to form a set of principles that would haunt and cloud my life forever. There were four chief principles that I did hold onto into my adulthood:

1. don't trust white males
2. America talks a good game, but doesn't play by the rules
3. help will forever be slow in coming (so you better help yourself)
4. learn the game first, master it, *then* you can change it

This was a sordid reality I had to live with as I came into manhood. My mother hinted at these realities, but she was much more positive. She taught empowerment principles.

Once you find what works for you, don't become inflexible, but run 'til the wheels fall off. There will come a time when game changers enter the picture; you must be ready to change. Change is not always bad, but it must have a positive objective. Anything other than that is worthless. I'll add also, short-term change is of little value.

I'm Just Sayin'

Back in 2013, I had the exhilarating opportunity to run for the DC City Council. I ran as not only a first-timer, but a true outsider. I ran solely based on Green Party principles—in one of America's most politically corrupt cites.

This is where principle rises to the surface. You see, DC is one of those cities seeing grand change—and not everybody is in on it. The nation's capitol is undergoing gentrification to the nth degree. The city leaders on the Council lead the charge. Regardless of the Ward a Council person represents, none of them fight for the people—the poor, Black and under-served people.

American Exceptionalism

What we've come to learn is that struggle in America is based upon someone **not** struggling. Some people call it, "haves and have nots." There is a faction of America that believes that they are entitled to all that America has to give—and if America isn't giving it, it must be taken. This is the concept of American Exceptionalism. The idea that I know what's best and what I want is what works best for you—all of you— and there is no debate about it. This mode of thinking is why we—Black people—struggle today.

This also speaks to the unrealistic concept of a "post-racial America." I get incensed whenever I hear that phrase bantered about. It takes pure sadism to ignore the fact that the richest country on earth has millions of it's citizens living in borderline and abject poverty. But one has to be able to deceive him/herself to still lay claim to being "exceptional." I trust no one who can do that.

American Exceptionalism refers to the theory that the United States is qualitatively different from other nation-states. In this view, America's Exceptionalism stems from its emergence from a revolution, becoming "the first new nation," and developing a uniquely American ideology, based on liberty, egalitarianism, individualism, populism and laissez-faire. This observation can be traced to Alexis de Tocqueville, the first writer to describe the United States as "exceptional" in 1831 and 1840. Once de Tocqueville put it out there, Americans hung onto it.

The idea that "I am different from you" is the basis for the inequalities of today. That idea was the basis for American slavery. This is the underlying foe in today's politics, policies, institutions and communications. This undercurrent is a curse on all of those who reside in America, regardless of one's station in life.

If one is well-to-do, then that person lives in fear of losing what he/she has. If one is poor, then they are relegated to a life of struggle. That is not to say that either of those two positions have to be permanent, but there are forces seeking to keep it permanent. The societal structure of inequality is perpetuated through the allocation of public funding, limitations placed on the education system, systemic gentrification and voter manipulation.

Each of these facets of social interaction are undergirded with race as the proposition that serves as the foundation for the chain of reasoning that unequal is alright. It is thought *reasonable* that Black unemployment is consistently double that of whites. It is reasoned *acceptable* that the top 1% of households (the upper class) owned 34.6% of all privately held wealth while the other 99% fight it out over the rest.

What does my assertion look like in practical terms? Well, Vermont Sen. Bernie Sanders, an independent who caucuses with Democrats, tweeted a startling statistic to his followers on July 22, 2012: "Today the Walton family of Wal-Mart own more wealth than the bottom 40% of America."

Sanders speaks and writes frequently about wealth distribution in the U.S., a hot-button issue among progressives and a rallying cry of the Occupy Wall Street Movement of 2011.

If you happen to be in that 1% (or less), then you are likely to strongly believe in American exceptionalism—that you are unlike everyone else. If you're not, then if you believe in American exceptionalism, then it's likely that you are a southerner, a Jew or an evangelical Christian. Factually speaking, all man is alike—with subtle differences. The essence of men are the same. We all must eat, defecate, procreate (or at least make the motions) and socialize. That's what we do. All else are man-inspired characteristics, including exceptionalism.

Although the term does not necessarily imply superiority, many neoconservative and American conservative writers have promoted its use in that sense. To them, the United States is like the biblical "shining city on a hill," and exempt from historical forces that have affected other countries. This country is one that "cannot fail" and "makes no mistake" in policy or principle. With that said, we can see the seeds that cause discord within our society—and the cause of struggle. That exceptionalism is relegated to a chosen few. Though it is propagandized for America as a nation, it is meant for a specific few.

Mitt Romney, as a presidential candidate in 2012 on a visit to Israel said that the Jewish state's economic success compared with its Palestinian neighbors, was due to "cultural" differences and the "hand of providence", implying exceptionalism. Of course, the statement angered many who see the reality of Israel's success as compared to Palestine: denial of its nationhood, military occupation and economic sanctions and blockades. That's an example of race-neutral exceptionalism looks like...based on principle.

In the immigration reform debate, whites in the southern border states want Mexican and Central American (they call them Mexicans too) peoples captured and deported; they want a fence at the border. Their position is America is meant for the ones already here. Of course, we can hear the exceptionalism in that position. If that was the case, the Europeans of Ellis Island should've been rounded up a long time ago! Not to mention, the states of California, Arizona, New Mexico, Texas, all belonged to the Mexican anyway!

I watched a PBS special[15] on the immigration debate where a white woman on a border picket line stands shouting at pro-immigrant Mexican protestors, "You lost the war!" This implies that whites are right—no matter the atrocity—and affirms the Columbus mentality: we decimated you and since you haven't done anything about it, suck it up...live with it! This is the battle that permeates division and maintains strife in America.

We observe a class and race of American that calls his/her stand "principle," to deny Mexicans entry into

America. What I find ironic is that they never mention the Russian or British immigrants (Piers Morgan, Simon Cowell, Sharon Osbourne, etc.). These people look like the complainers, so we know that the issue is not immigration, but race.

This contradiction on immigration is how principle can be contorted and stifle your freedom.

This chapter is the most dangerous chapter in the book, because it can be so contradictory. Standing on principle isn't always what it's cracked up to be. If it works for you, then you perceive it as right; but if someone else's principle works *against* you, then you have two choices: one, concede to theirs, or two, re-define what principle is and should be. Just because someone "stands on principle" doesn't mean you shouldn't stand on yours. It also doesn't mean that yours aren't right.

Principle is defined as a fundamental truth or proposition that serves as the foundation for a system of belief or behavior or for a chain of reasoning; a rule or belief governing one's personal behavior. Knowing this, there's no wonder everyone believes they are right.

Chapter Five

As A Condition of Your Freedom, You Cannot...
Become the Thing That You Hate

"Success, recognition, and conformity are the bywords of the modern world where everyone seems to crave the anesthetizing security of being identified with the majority."
        ~Martin Luther King, Jr., *Strength to Love*, 1963

This is among the toughest chapters to write. Neo-conservatism and Tea Party politics of the late-2000's have clearly become the inflammatory tool that Klansmen, Birchers and Buckley-ites intended it to be. With every turn, I am tempted to "fight fire with fire." Fire has turned out to be an effective tool for rooting out the enemy (ask the Klu Klux Klan!).

There's another issue that needs to be put on front street...Black people being lulled into acting like whites—for whatever reason. This is unacceptable, though many accept it as, "being American." And for the record, what does that mean? Let me illustrate...

Where we as a society, have been conditioned to hold fast to a moral view that it is an "abomination" (a word one will only use when they're trying to sound "holier-than-thou") to accept the lifestyle choice of someone else. We have come to find in our country's contemporary history that some of the very people we admired most and revered greatest were closet gays.

How utterly surprised we were...or acted, when the truth came out.

Marv Albert, former New Jersey Governor Jim McGreevey, Pastor Ted Haggard, etc., were being what we wanted while we, as a society, had them scared to death to be themselves. One thing for sure, if anyone needs not be afraid of being themselves—even in the face of the worst onslaught of pretentious white people—are Blacks.

I wrote a Socially Speaking commentary on that very issue in June of 2011:

I've got some friends who claim to be "men of God." I dare doubt them, but I listen and watch their belief and rhetoric in action...especially, the Christian ones. I've been having some heavy conversations with those peers about an issue that is and will be front-burner in the socio-political arena: gay rights. The majority of my peers are working-class and black folks. Most of them are totally against bestowing "civil rights" on gays and lesbians. I challenge them using an irrefutable tool: their faith.

We've argued about what gays should be allowed to do in our society: fight in the military, get married to each other, adopt children or preach in the pulpit. There are a host of other activities that I broach after my peers holler "no" to each one. They usually stand firm in their positions until I remind them of the icon of their faith.

I bring to the table the acts of grace and redemption practiced by a man named Jesus. Some call him a "savior of the world," others, a prophet. But whatever the case, he is arguably the most recalled human to ever walk the earth. More books referencing him have been written (same narrative too!) than any other manuscript, so that should give his words some degree of credibility.

I remind them that, as a holy man—or "man of God"—he sat down with the tax collectors and prostitutes. He commanded—as a condition of salvation—that men everywhere ought to forgive other men for their "failures." That men are commanded—by God—to accept people right where they are...and as they are.

More relevant beyond the spiritual aspect is the social piece: that poor people—that black people—don't ever want to become the thing that they hate. Acting as racists do is unacceptable. People afflicted by discrimination cannot make way to "do as the Romans."

I'm straight, but that has nothing to do with what other people choose. I can't choose [straightness] for them. I caution the men I mentor that "you can't make anyone do anything." If you spend your energy thinking about changing someone else, the best way to do that is to do what you do—if it's allegedly right!

Opponents of gay marriage are challenging the principle of judicial neutrality in San Francisco. In a courtroom this week, they're arguing that a federal judge who struck down California's ban on same sex marriage last year was biased because he's in a same-sex relationship. That's got to be the most insane arguments one could make!

As the trial challenging California's Proposition 8 got under way last year, media began reporting that the federal judge overseeing the case was gay. No one would "openly" say anything, but they threw it out there. It never came up during the proceedings, but a few months ago, as Judge Vaughn Walker was retiring from the bench, he spilled the beans. He told the press that he was in a long-term relationship with another man.

"Judge Walker's 10-year same-sex relationship creates this unavoidable impression that he was just not the impartial judge that the law requires," says Andrew Pugno, one of the attorneys defending Proposition 8. The issue here isn't Judge Walker's sexual orientation — not exactly — but rather that his relationship left him in the same shoes as two same-sex couples who wanted to get married, said Pugno. Now, isn't that special...

Let me get this straight...the logic is that if you're gay and have to rule on a gay issue and you rule for the gays, then you're biased? Okay, using that logic, let me replace the noun with another noun: if you're straight and have to rule on a straight issue and you rule for the straight, then you're **not** biased? Or better yet, if you're a white male and have to rule on a white, male issue and you rule for the white, male, then you're biased? Of course not, it doesn't make sense to you either...

Black people can be as prejudice as they want. Everyone is. What they can't be is discriminatory. Blacks are the most despised beings in this country. Whites will choose dogs over Negroes! Whites cut social services from municipal budgets and close homeless shelters, while they build dog parks in our city with taxpayer money. For all of those who think racism is dead and that discrimination is passé, get real. Whites are unabashedly repealing all legislation that remotely evened the playing field. Out of the

535 members of the 112thcongress, there are 42 Black people—and you think everything is fair? That's 8% of the whole when we are 12% of the nation's population.

I said all of that to say this: if you're fighting for a voice; if you are fighting for your rights, then why would you deny someone else theirs? How "godly" is that? Just because you disagree with how someone else runs their lives, don't think for a minute that you want someone else running yours...'cause you don't! If you don't want a gay marriage, then don't get one. More importantly than that, don't become the thing that you hate. You surely wouldn't want anyone putting you in that bag.

It is really easy for me to deliver "an eye for an eye." There was a period of my life where I did just that. I robbed *white* people—and businesses—solely as retribution for the wrongs that they had collectively done to me in my life. I stole their cars and threatened their lives...a one man wrecking crew. When it was reported on the evening news, the reporter would say, "The suspect was a lone white man." I was, at that time, satisfied. My spirit wasn't filled, but the carnal man in me felt vindicated.

For the time in 1981 at 16-years old, that I was confronted and my life threatened on the railroad track behind Whitfield Chapel apartments in Lanham, Maryland or the time I was told, "this is a white man's army" in 1983 at Fort Campbell, Kentucky, I vowed to have my day.

This went on for maybe ten years. Sometime, I got caught, even if for the wrong thing. God has a way of working that out. What I learned is that you'll pay for whatever you do. As in the law, your reasons have no bearing on your guilt. In coming to that realization, it dawned on me that it applied to others too.

My calculated and precise acts of violence, aggression and retribution served to show me the worthlessness in the value of "things." What society valued, was of little consequence. Each item with a dollar value attached to it was replaceable. Whites had the resources to do that. Each bank bag that I pilfered, was insured somewhere along the line. Whites had the resources to do that. I began to realize that wealth and worth was bigger than the seeing eye.

Sure, I ate well for a period and I paid bills that were due because of those acts of aggression, but the lasting effects of my strikes on their wealth was of little consequence. I scared the hell out of several white men. I found that that was my underlying objective. Yet, the bigger problem wasn't being solved by my acts. That's when I began to equate my actions with those of the nation. We call it peace, but it's really violence. I had become the thing that I hated.

I implore the people I encounter to not take on the characteristics of their tormentor. Many, in the context of their replies, don't know who their tormentor is! That always stuns me—for just a second—then I share...

In issues of economics, housing, employment, contracting, education, governance, Blacks who have gained a higher degree of elevation, have morphicized into the systemic problem-maker. They have essentially become the thing that they hate.

I wrote a song some years ago on that very issue. After struggling with the theory of social change activists that Black people can't be racist, I concluded that my position had credence. The idea that "power + prejudice = racism" is pretty much accurate, but not necessarily full. I agree that systemically, power is the necessary element to execute institutional racism, but many who are victimized by racism aren't even aware that they are in a system!

Racism can be compartmentalized, effectually demoralizing and degrading an individual's quality of life. In the 2001 composition, "Black Racist", I write:

I've heard it said in the land of the dead
that a man won't always swallow what a man is fed;
but then there're two points of view:
what he's feeding him and what he's feeding you...
My experience, what he fed me is crap—told me to
rise while he stabbed me in the back;
"you can succeed if you just give your all"...what he
didn't tell you: what'll happen when you fall...
Black Racist...
Time for me to lay my chips on the table; any Black
man would've taken Betty Grable...over Dorothy
Dandridge—but that's what the plan is: implant our
minds and use our time with images other than
mine; but rather me use yours—and make my
momma's daughters whores, and then slant the
score, and make you want more...ironing board
behind, blonde hair, thin lips, blue eyes...
and grow to despise where you come from and make
you want some...some of what'll never ever make
you part of the plan: 2/3s of a man...and now you're
pissed—so you dissed—another brother that
resemble this Black racist.
That's one lesson, let me teach you another one:
now you're moving up just like the Jeffersons...

Driving your Benzo, work for Nippendeso—making a
living wage, counting your 401k...

Now for your children, you do what's best, pick up sticks, and move out west...and forget where you come from; now you're a small fish in a big pond—when you could've change the city government's wand...that they wave—as you watch your old high school deteriorate and decay...Black Racist.
Oh, I know, "Redd, what you talkin' 'bout? Don't be hatin' "cause I got me some clout!" My brother, you don't get it: once you realize you're Black, don't have a fit. 'Cause they made you head-nigger-in-charge—and let you drive their head nigger cars...

Then you follow the slavery script; even if it's wrong you'll put up with it, 'cause you don't wanna lose your shit...but then they tell you to fire your friend—and he ain't even done nothing' wrong...but it was way too many Blacks in this song...Black Racist.

Factually speaking, we've been sold a bill of goods. That the "American Dream" is for all people. That Constitution of the United States is for all people. Upon ratification in 1788, the Constitution was designed for the citizenry of the country—at that time. Blacks we not citizens, therefore, it was not designed, nor written, for Blacks. That's why we struggle so heavily. That's why we've been perpetually playing catch up.

Whether politically, economically or socially, Blacks are and have been foreigners in this land. As such, we understand that whites have a grand desire to keep it that way...if you were on top, wouldn't you? With that established, we move to the next relevant point: is that just and right? Any human being with a scintilla of decency would day "no." Next logical question is, do I become right or wrong. Most of us will answer, right—unless someone throws money into the equation. We know from The Bible, that satan offer riches to Jesus if he would ride with him. That's what's happened to Blacks in America. For the sake of dollar bills, Blacks will become the thing that they hate.

They will disenfranchise, deny rights, cut entitlements and outright hate against the very people they are. Where their status is threatened—with equality or abolishment alike—they will act like the white oppressor, i.e., racist.

Don't get me wrong, they don't make an impact on the system, per se, but they do make an impact of people within that system—the victims. They create more victims and perpetuate the evil work of the oppressors—even absent institutional power. They are the faces of racism.

I was on Facebook one day after the state-sanctioned murder of Georgia death row inmate, Troy Davis. I came across a comment from a young Black brother:

> Here [are] my thoughts on the Troy Davis Death Penalty case. "An ounce of prevention will prevent you from getting killed."
> - Jamil A. Hill

I cannot begin to tell you how incensed I was by Mr. Hill's view of handling racist policy. Then, I realized that in the unconscious mind of a Black man in America, this is the prevailing view: go along, to get along. I responded to Mr. Hill:

> I don't agree; injustice is a predator. One cannot sleep his/her life away...all one must do is walk, drive or breath while being Black in America--and the system will find you. Whether its housing, employment or criminal justice, one doesn't HAVE to

be guilty to be handed injustice. Don't get it twisted,
I know. I had to fight to have my case overturned
and eventually acquitted--and I **wasn't** guilty.

Others chimed in abrasive to the Mr. Hill's position; he
responded with:

You'll missing the Big Picture! We need to get our
Shit Together. Evidently, we still believe we are
doing it Right. We don't even love ourselves to tell
someone when we know they're doing wrong.
Weather its Child Support, Stealing, Robbing, Drug
Dealing, Killing, etc. If we knew better then we'd do
better.

Rightly so, a gentleman named Reggie Jenkins added
to the conversation:

Jamil, we are talking about TROY, he didn't steal or
commit any offenses. True we need to be more
accountable, but let's stop pretending that we are
not at war. Black males are the target. We need to
cut out this 'holier than thou' mindset,...I know it
goes deeper but we need to crawl before we walk.
500 years of self-hatred is a mighty thing to get
over. But me & you know the truth but many people
can't handle the truth.

I just couldn't let that piece lie out there:

...and remember: truth should never be in the eyes
of the beholder, but in the facts of the collective.
Whites are a good example of making up their own
"truth" (i.e., "Columbus discovered America"); just
because someone SAYS it's true, doesn't mean it is
(i.e., Troy Davis' guilt).

Later in the thread, I added:

Brother Jamil, I don't subscribe to the "blame the victim" mentality. We—just like other races of people—have to be responsible for our own behavior. There is no argument there. Davis' killing was rooted in a system designed to fail. Unfortunately, the legacy that we, as Black men, live with is littered by systemic injustice perpetuated by the keepers of the gate. Michelle Alexander's "The New Jim Crow" expounds scholarly on what that looks like in both its practical and legal from. We always wanted to get along...whites wanted us to get down—I refuse to bow.

To the point of this chapter, if you want to be free, you must be relieved of all guilt. Mr. Hill termed it, "self-hate." We, Blacks in America, did not cause this condition and are not responsible for racism. Since you are here, you must adhere to the premise that you have a right—and stake—in this country; in its successes and/or failures.

The Constitution was amended to include you, thus you have a right and stake in this country's policies and condition. It's screwed up, but that's not your doing; it was like that when you gained your citizenship—whether upon birth or arrival (one in the same?). Do not subscribe to the mentality of racist, imperialist, capitalist oppressors...it's bad for your mental, spiritual and overall health.

Language

We cannot adopt the language of the oppressor class. It demeans, miseducates and degrades our struggle for social and economic parity. Language is among the most important tools used by the oppressors to keep those lower classes in submission.

There are many instances in the political arena where the common man is deceived out of his own self-interests through simple language frames: Clean Coal, the Clean Skies Act, Obamacare, The Defense of Marriage Act. Let's use Affirmative Action; a very positive term on its face. Underneath, the objectives are indeed noble and fair...to those who are routinely and systemically denied social and economic opportunities in America. Affirmative Action was legislated as remedial action for a racial injustice.

But there were and are opponents to the legislation who continuously claim that it's time has passed, because we have "solved" the race problem in America. Nothing could be farther from the truth. Factually speaking, there are those that oppose Affirmative Action and term the practice as "quotas." That's deceptive and meant to be.

Language is among the most important elements of political discourse. One of my mentors, Professor George Lakoff speaks directly on what he calls "framing": frames do not have to fit the facts, but must create a recognizable mental picture that people can visualize—and must achieve your objective.

Let me share a real life example that still embeds a grand resentment for me to this day against my adopted hometown, Knoxville, Tennessee.

A dear friend of mine, the late Councilman Danny Mayfield passed away on March 21, 2001. Filling his vacant seat was a hot topic in the city. Mayfield's City Council colleagues were among several hundred mourners who attended a memorial service at Greater Warner Tabernacle AME Zion Church, where the Mayfields were active members of the congregation.

Among the speakers was Carlene Malone, the colleague to whom he was closest, and Republican Mayor Victor Ashe, who said he had developed a warm personal relationship with Knoxville's youngest Council member, despite the fact that Mayfield ran against him two years prior. He praised Mayfield for his Christian convictions and courage in the face of death. Greater Warner minister Rev. Eric Leake warned of "a cancer on this city" and denounced those who had been watching for Mayfield to die because they wanted his Council seat.

Many in the city, especially in the activist community, advocated vigorously for Mayfield's wife Melissa, to fill his seat and complete his term. There were forces working just as vigorously to make sure that wouldn't happen.

It is fair to say that Danny Mayfield, whose first order of business as a new Council member in 1997 was to push for a police review board in the wake of the deaths of several Black Americans, was unpopular with the KPD administration and with some officers. I know a little something about that, but that's a different book.

Tribe One, a street ministry Mayfield founded along with his partner, subsequent City Councilman Chris Woodhull, was viewed with skepticism by some KPD brass, who referred to the organization by the derisive nickname "Hug-A-Thug." That moniker stuck in the minds of many Knoxvillians—while the city's conservatives painted the frame in people's minds by using it as if that was the official name of a program.

This deceptive use of language caused great and unwarranted challenges to a Tribe One agenda that benefitted many poor and under-privileged young people in the city. What's even more unfortunate, to the untrained, non-politically-attuned mind, they believed it.

What I share with you is that I refuse to share a conversation, a panel or a debate with anyone (usually a white male) who uses the term "thug" when referring to people they don't like (usually Black males). That framed term as used a racist label to exempt them from using the N-word.

This tact is successful and used more and more often in politics and subsequently, in commonspeak among the people. Among the populace, we know it's wrong, immoral and unethical, but we also know that it works. We know that "everybody does it." But one more thing we know: that it's not right.

Martin Luther King, Jr. said, "On some positions, cowardice asks the question, "Is it safe?" Expediency asks the question, "Is it politic?" And Vanity comes along and asks the question, "Is it popular?" But Conscience asks the question "Is it right?" And there comes a time when one must take a position that is neither safe, nor politic, nor popular, but he must do it because Conscience tells him it is right." You know what it is. Don't become the thing that you hate.

Chapter Six

As A Condition of Your Freedom, You Cannot...
Sit It Out

"I am working for the time when unqualified blacks, browns, and women join the unqualified men in running our government."

~Cissy Farenthold

If you think that you don't have a dog in that fight, then you're asking for that dog to eventually bite you. Whichever dog wins will heal and then look for the next one to devour. That next one may be you.

Just remember the famous statement attributed to pastor Martin Niemöller (1892–1984) about the inactivity of German intellectuals following the Nazi rise to power and the purging of their chosen targets, group after group:

"First they came for the communists, and I didn't speak out because I wasn't a communist.
Then they came for the trade unionists, and I didn't speak out because I wasn't a trade unionist.
Then they came for the Jews, and I didn't speak out because I wasn't a Jew.
Then they came for me and there was no one left to speak out for me."

I get highly agitated at men who believe that politics don't matter. One of the most important facets of one's American existence is not only politically

connected, but because of politics. For Black Americans, that is more intricately the case.
Many a Black says that they want to be rich and that capitalism is an appropriate means in which to get there. What they fail to see is that they are *not* rich. I don't know of a single person who came from my neighborhood who has landed on the Forbes 500 list of richest Americans. That fact has nothing to do with my neighborhood, per se, but the fact that America has designed capitalism toward that result.

In the United States, wealth is highly concentrated in a relatively few hands. As of 2007, the top 1% of households (the upper class) owned 34.6% of all privately held wealth, and the next 19% (the managerial, professional, and small business stratum) had 50.5%, which means that just 20% of the people owned a remarkable 85%, leaving only 15% of the wealth for the bottom 80% (wage and salary workers). In terms of financial wealth (total net worth minus the value of one's home), the top 1% of households had an even greater share: 42.7%.[16]

The wealth gaps between whites and minorities have grown to their widest levels in a quarter-century. The recession and *uneven* recovery have erased decades of minority gains, leaving whites on average with 20 times the net worth of blacks and 18 times that of Hispanics, according to an analysis of relatively new Census data.

The 2011 analysis shows the racial and ethnic impact of the economic meltdown, which ravaged housing values and sent unemployment soaring. It offers the most direct government evidence yet of the disparity between predominantly younger minorities whose main asset is their home and older whites who are more likely to have 401(k) retirement accounts or other stock holdings.

More importantly, the dynamic of racial disparity plays the greater part in the reason one cannot isolate himself.

When it comes to identifying issues that create and contribute to ongoing wealth inequality in the United States, it is also important to observe issues that surround the disparity in wealth between different racial groups. Upon observation of wealth inequality in the United States it is obvious that there remains to this day a large wealth gap between whites and Black Americans.

This gap could be from a variety of things however the most important when evaluating this topic is inheritance. Inheritance refers to the amount of unused material possessions and assets that can be transferred from previous generations to future generations.

Inheritance therefore takes on a special meaning when considering the wealth gap between blacks and whites in today's world because it can directly link the disadvantaged economic position and prospects of today's blacks to the disadvantaged positions of their parents' and grandparents' generations. According to a report done by Robert B. Avery and Michael S. Rendall, [17]one in three white households will receive a substantial inheritance during their lifetime compared to only one in ten black households.

This lack of inheritance that has been observed among Black Americans could be caused by a number of reasons. Racial differences in family background could be a potentially important cause in disparities of inheritance. It has been observed that there are clear differences in the family structure between whites and minorities. Specifically it has been found that there is increased fertility and family size among Blacks as compared to whites. This could possibly explain the disparity in inheritance because an increase in family size would statistically result in a greater strain on the family's resources.

Since more resources are required to meet the family's needs in the present, there would be fewer resources allocated to each family member in future periods. Furthermore since minorities typically have larger families any leftover resources would be divided between a larger group of people and would result in a diminished inheritance.

This theory is too much like sense, that's why most white Americans dismiss it as baseless. The traditional mindset is trained to think that effort is the sole determiner of wealth. What I know is that there is power in numbers; but that power is diminished if those numbers are divided, separate or dormant. Whites know this. That is why they pollute the American psyche with American Idol, reality TV shows and entertainment industry gossip. We get distracted from the thing that matters: decision-making concerning your welfare.

The people who would prefer you sit it out are the very ones who are doing the best. The median wealth of white U.S. households in 2009 was $113,149, compared with $6,325 for Hispanics and $5,677 for blacks, according to the analysis released in July 2011 by the Pew Research Center.[18] Those ratios, roughly 20-to-1 for blacks and 18-to-1 for Hispanics, far exceed the low mark of 7-to-1 for both groups reached in 1995, when the nation's economic expansion lifted many low-income groups to the middle class.

The white-black wealth gap is also the widest since the census began tracking such data in 1984, when the ratio was roughly 12-to-1.

Commerce matters, but civil rights matter more. One cannot participate substantially in the commerce of a society if one is disenfranchised; because every dollar he/she makes is subject to be taken if he/she is treated as less than a man.

I was blessed to witness a movement born in America. There were several during my lifetime: the Civil Rights Movement, The Black Power Movement, The Million Man March. Each involved Black people at the core. In 2009, I saw the rise of the Tea Party, which was well defined, well designed (and well-funded). It was mean-spirited and targeted, much like the Black Power movement. The Tea Party was based in fear and anger.

Then I witnessed and joined the Occupy Wall Street movement. A leaderless metamorphosis of people seeking the same moral imperative: justice. One that was long overdue.

This movement, like each one passed, was demonized, vilified and criticized by the status quo and the power elite—the rich. Those attacks gave the movement credibility. There had to be something to it if the white males attacked it, right?

I'll never forget during the early stages of the Occupy Wall Street protests, the Republicans maligned it; Newt Gingrich, said that they needed to "get a job and take a bath." Scared to death, the Democrats ignored it. The media questioned it (as opposed to reporting on it). To its credit, it changed the conversation about wealth disparity.

Occupy Wall Street was a spirited and leaderless protest in the Wall Street section of New York that started in September 2011 and had inspired a growing number of demonstrations across the world.

The protests began on September 17[th]as hundreds of people descended on the streets of Manhattan's financial district. Since then, the movement had spread to dozens of other cities. And, on October 15, the movement went global with protests in dozens of countries.

The movement, which was modeled after social-media-driven demonstrations in the Middle East, aimed to raise awareness about the role financial institutions played in the continued economic downturn affecting the world markets, and to show their discontent at the lukewarm attempts to prosecute those at fault. Demonstrators also rallied against the state of the war in Afghanistan, the state of the environment, and a wide array of other domestic and international issues.

Occupy Wall Street was a leaderless resistance movement which included people of many colors, genders and political persuasions. The one thing they all had in common is that they were "The 99%" that elected to no longer tolerate the greed and corruption of the 1% of Americans. They used the revolutionary Arab Spring tactic to achieve their ends and encourage the use of nonviolence to maximize the safety of all participants.

They occupied Wall Street—and then all across the nation. From San Francisco to New York; from Austin, Texas to Washington, DC, "occupations" were formed. Politicians were uncertain of how to react. Most were clumsy and downright un-American in their positions on the Occupy movement. Some tried to toe the line between their constituencies and their corporate donors.

Mayor Michael R. Bloomberg, speaking on the day that Occupy Wall Street protesters marked their one-month anniversary in Zuccotti Park, said he was trying to strike a balance between protecting protesters' right to free speech and the needs of Lower Manhattan residents.

"The Constitution doesn't protect tents," he said at a news conference in Queens. "It protects speech and assembly." This absolutely senseless logic is like saying that when the Tea Party movement protested in April of 2010, "The Constitution doesn't protect flags and stages." Real simple, the artifacts and propaganda we bring to rallies and protest symbolize our "free speech."

Bloomberg expressed concern that those exercising a "right to be silent" might be getting drowned out amid the din of the protests. How can you know if they're silent? And if they choose to remain silent, then they're exercising that right pretty well!

"We can't have a place where only one point of view is allowed," he said. "There are places where I think it's appropriate to express yourself, and there are other places that are appropriate to set up Tent City. They don't necessarily have to be one and the same." This was an insane bit of logic that probably was formulated in the Americans for Tax Reform's Wednesday meetings...

I posited on my radio show that week, that there were parks other than Zucotti where opposing views could be spouted. If another group wanted to set up tent cities in *support* of America resisting the fiscal rape by Wall Street, then they had every right to do so.

Occupy Wall Street had proven successful in one thing for certain: getting the grievance of the true American people—the 99%--on the map. The Right-wing had claimed and propagandized in the prior two years that the Tea Party was the voice of the people, but what we saw was that the Tea Party's complaints had little to no positive effect on the everyday working class American: food, shelter and clothing. That's what Occupy Wall Street was about. People who were affected didn't sit it out.

In contrast, the Tea Party's gripes impacted and benefitted big business, Wall Street and the war machine. The Tea Party masqueraded as "the people", but turned out to be anything but...and sadly, most Tea Party participants didn't even know it.

The conservative Right had put out their attack lines, and put their demonization script to work. They'd come up with outrageousness from anti-Americanism claims from top-tier Republican presidential candidate, Herman Cain to the elementary name-calling of Evangelist Pat Robertson.

If the tea party was a conservative response to President Barack Obama's economic bailout plan in the spring of 2009, Occupy Wall Street came about partly due to progressives' reaction to the outcome of summer 2010's acrimonious debt-ceiling debate. Obama and other top Democrats ultimately agreed to over $2 trillion in spending cuts without any tax hikes on Wall Street financiers or others considered responsible for the economic crisis.

Code Word: "Mob"

The House Majority Leader at the time, Eric Cantor (R-Va) used part of his address to the Values Voters

Summit in Washington, DC to attack the Occupy Wall Street protests, and he condemned political leaders who were supporting them. The public couldn't gravitate toward this position. Stealing from the American public for personal gain needed to be rebuffed by elected leaders.

But what was most damning, was when the fear card got played by Cantor, speaking on behalf of the conservative right—who were defending the rich: "This administration's failed policies have resulted in an assault on many of our nation's bedrock principles," he said. "If you read the newspapers today, I, for one, am increasingly concerned about the growing mobs occupying Wall Street and the other cities across the country. And believe it or not, some in this town, have actually condoned the pitting of Americans against Americans. But you sent us here to fight for you and all Americans."

Then why wasn't he fighting *for* the Occupy Wall Streeters? Protesters voicing their disagreement with governmental policies was who the Tea Party was in 2010; Protesters voicing their disagreement with governmental policies was a "mob" when Occupy Wall Street did it in 2011. My, how time changes things...

But when he spoke at the Values Voter Summit in 2009, Cantor expressed a very different sentiment toward another movement that was arguably "pitting Americans against Americans" -- the Tea Party.

This group of "activists" wanted to "Take Our Country Back." The pronoun "our" is indicative of "us versus them." This was a welcomed pitting of Americans against Americans. No other way to look at it. Conveniently, Cantor forgot about that.

The Occupy Wall Street movement was a defining moment in America's *story* at the time. The economy was in a recession, unemployment was over 9%, President Obama was trying to pass a jobs bill (when incidentally, in the previous months the Republicans accused Obama of not giving attention to the jobs problem). The Republicans said no to everything Obama attempted to do. But the people—the majority of Americans—chose not to sit it out.

Poll after poll showed that a plurality of Americans agreed with the premise of the Occupy movement: that somebody (the 1%) stole the money and 99% of Americans are paying the price for it. The protest that had spread from Lower Manhattan to as far as Rome and Hong Kong, was supported by most New Yorkers, according to a Quinnipiac University survey in October of 2011.[19]

Sixty-seven percent of New York City voters said they agree with the protesters' views, while 23 percent didn't, the school's Polling Institute said. Support ranged from 81 percent among registered Democrats to 58 percent among independents and 35 percent from Republicans. By 72 percent to 24 percent, voters said law-abiding demonstrators could stay as long as they wanted. It only made sense.

The reasons for the Occupy protests were obvious, though conservative pundits were persistent in mis-characterizing the movement as directionless. I made a sign that I carried to the

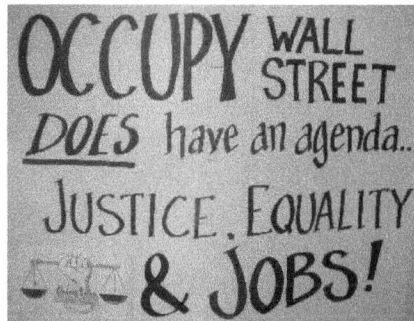

OCCUPY WALL STREET _DOES_ have an agenda... JUSTICE. EQUALITY & JOBS!

October 15th Jobs and Justice March on Washington called by Rev. Al Sharpton that answered the critics:

"Occupy Wall Street <u>does</u> have an agenda: justice, equality & jobs." Someone from the media interviewed me during the rally and asked what do you all want?

I responded that there would be no narrow demands, giving those charged with legislating, a means of marginalizing those demands. Demands mean that you can choose to do something or not do something. There is no choice here. We tell them the problem and force them to solve it. Either you fix it or we will...they are the legislators—do it!

Still, American media was playing dumb; acting as if they could find the basis for the Occupy movement. William K. Black articulated the problem concisely in his 2005 book, *"The Best Way to Rob a Bank Is to Own One: How Corporate Executives and Politicians Looted the S&L Industry."*[20] In it, he tells the story, much like Danny Schecter's documentary, *"Plundered."*

The catastrophic collapse of companies such as Enron, WorldCom, ImClone, and Tyco left angry investors, employees, reporters, and government investigators demanding to know how the CEOs deceived everyone into believing their companies were spectacularly successful when in fact they were massively insolvent. Why did the nation's top accounting firms give such companies clean audit reports? Where were the regulators and whistleblowers who should expose fraudulent CEOs before they loot their companies for hundreds of millions of dollars?

In this expert insider's account of the savings and loan debacle of the 1980s, William Black laid bare the strategies that corrupt CEOs and CFOs—in collusion with those who have regulatory oversight of their industries—used to defraud companies for their personal gain.

Recounting the investigations he conducted as Director of Litigation for the Federal Home Loan Bank Board, Black fully reveals how Charles Keating and hundreds of other S&L owners took advantage of a weak regulatory environment to perpetrate accounting fraud on a massive scale. He also authoritatively linked the S&L crash to the business failures of the early 2000s, showing how CEOs then and now are using the same tactics to defeat regulatory restraints and commit the same types of destructive fraud...and why Elizabeth Warren ran for the Massachusetts Senate seat in 2012.

William Black uses the latest advances in criminology and economics to develop a theory of why "control fraud"—looting a company for personal profit—tends to occur in waves that make financial markets deeply inefficient. He also explained how to prevent such waves. Throughout the book, Black drove home the larger point that control fraud is a major, ongoing threat in business that requires active, independent regulators to contain it. His book is a wake-up call for everyone who believes that market forces alone will keep companies and their owners honest.

Even with this knowledge out there, America allowed it to happen again. Since it happened again, the American people—the ones hurt the most by it—chose not to sit it out.

What I know is that when you are your most effective, the ones who sit within the status quo will demean you, question your motives rather than the issue you illuminate and will paint a dirty picture of you for others to see. I know.

During the late 1990's, Knoxville police were killing Black men in the Black community, East Knoxville. A band of citizens finally said enough is enough. A group formed, Citizens for Police Review. Though they were not the first in the country to do it, they were revolutionary for a southern city.

One of my mentors, Ron Davis asked my organization members to join them in this mission of bringing the police to accountability. My co-founders, Terry Taylor and the late Theresa Reed and I joined CPR. But we had a more immediate objective: stopping the murders of Black men at the hands of police.

Since I was an early believer in the power of personal video cameras, I suggested a plan to the group: to camcord the police on their automobile stops of Black men in our community. It just so happened that a reporter from the Knoxville News-Sentinel was there on an unrelated matter. He reported our intention to record the police.[21]

This got it in the media and the city was in an uproar. Before we knew it, the Fraternal Order of Police was on TV opposing our program. They brought out fears that had nothing to do with the program. They effectively scared the hell out of the public...that was their goal.

The media gave CPR a chance to respond, and interviewed me. I explained the genesis, basis, safeguards and objectives of our program. I thought that would end the controversy, especially since we had the Constitutional right to conduct our action.

It wasn't over by a long shot. The then-Chief-of-Police, Phil Keith, then targeted me! I wasn't even the focus of the program, but that's how the status quo operates. They aim to distract from their illicit acts.

Keith brought out to the public the fact that I was a formerly convicted felon. My 1991 conviction for an unproven armed robbery earned me a page long expose in the News-Sentinel. It scared my community; but it also brought out many who supported, not only our program, but people who had met and worked with me. It galvanized our community. Blacks knew what "black-balling" a person looked like. It was a moment in my early activism where the people didn't sit it out.

And therein, lies my point. We cannot sit it out. Blacks cannot believe that Occupy Wall Street—or any other movement to right the scales—is not *their* business. You know the old saying: "when white America catches a cold, Black America gets the flu!" Its all relative. If you don't act when it's someone else, there'll be no one around to act when its you...'cause they shall come for you!

Factually speaking, the Occupy movement was 40 years late. Blacks have been "occupying for decades, if not centuries. Just look at the Civil Rights Movement...

OWS wouldn't have even been born had not the white middle class been adversely affected. The issues of high unemployment, lack of government resources and corporate profits while cutting working class benefits and protections were always problems that blacks had endured. Not that blacks liked it, but the oversight entities proved unwilling to enforce laws that prevented these behaviors which led to the collapse of the American economy.

The Occupy Wall Street movement presented an opportunity for Blacks to re-light fires under issues of immediate concern: mass incarceration, unemployment and societal exclusion. Unlike the Occupy movement, Blacks didn't have to be vague in articulating their issues. Quite the opposite; it was imperative that the Black community "call a spade a spade." Nothing will get done for Blacks in America if you don't tell whites what shall be done.

Don't get me wrong, I know how frustrating it can be when you see injustice go unpunished again and again. I re-present the case of federal court judge Samuel B. Kent. Who on May 11, 2009, was sentenced to 33 months in prison in a sex abuse case for lying to investigators about sexually abusing two female employees. Dick DeGuerin, Kent's attorney, said the judge was retiring from the bench because of a disability—which would allow him to keep receiving his $169,300-a-year salary. How utterly convenient— and criminal, because, retired federal judges collect their full salaries for the remainder of their lives; judges who resign get nothing. Kent found it convenient to all of a sudden, claim a disability.

What's criminal is that somebody wrote that into law— made it legal! We deny disable people health care and social security, the country is in a recession and rich people keep getting paid! And we can't keep homeless shelters open?

In democratic societies, change comes through organizing and voting. If you want to see change, you've got to be it. It's not for someone else to do. My god-brother is one of those who has benefitted from the sacrifices of others, but is never compelled to do the same for others yet to come. He rests well in his comfortability, in blissful ignorance that they— white males—can come get that at any time.

Martin King said, "Change does not roll in on the wheels of inevitability, but comes through continuous struggle. And so we must straighten our backs and work for our freedom. A man can't ride you unless your back is bent." They will ride your back as long as you let 'em. They have no shame in doing so. Can't be said any other way...you can't sit it out.

Chapter Seven

As A Condition of Your Freedom, You Cannot...
Wait for God

"Past the seeker as he prayed came the crippled and the beggar and the beaten. And seeing them... he cried, "Great God, how is it that a loving creator can see such things and yet do nothing about them?" God said, "I did do something. I made you."

~Author Unknown

I guess I'll start this chapter with 12 qualifiers of definition:

1. I believe in God
2. I believe in <u>one</u> God—in three characters
3. I believe in Jesus
4. I believe Jesus
5. I once pastored a church
6. I believe that man has screwed with God's word and intent to benefit the dominant class
7. I believe Christians are crazy
8. I believe that God loves and saves all the people of his/her creation
9. I believe God is not sexist, nor is gender specific
10. I don't believe that God *chose* the Jews
11. I don't believe that God saves everybody...some people don't need to be saved!
12. I believe in an unequivocal separation between church and state

Now, with that said, you will be able to more aptly grasp the self-redemptive wisdom I have for you. In this vein, you won't be prohibited by dogma or denominationalism. If we get those pieces out of the way, we prevent any and all proselytizing. I am not trying to convert you to anything and won't be mad if you choose to go to hell...just read my book first.

I am American by birth, and now, by choice. Later, I may very well choose otherwise, but in the meantime, I am an American (I realize that there are those who claim they are *no longer* Americans, but haven't left yet). The ills of America concern me and thus I speak to those things. I believe you should too, but you probably don't. You are very likely one who has gone along to get along. As we age, we realize that we are unfulfilled, because others have partaken in the American Dream and you are still trying.

In that realization, frustration over your status and reflection of your contribution has set in. You may be one of the many Americans who are just glad that you still have a job, home, and car...that no tragic situation has beset you. The best thing for you to do is be quiet and live—'til you die. How utterly pathetic of you. You'll get it later...

If you are one of those people, then simply proceed to the next chapter. This chapter is solely for those who desire their freedom—and willing to do something about getting it.

I am of the mind that mega-churches are for cowards. There is nothing more pathetic than a person who finds his/her strength in being a minnow in the sea. Staying unnoticed is humility, but that existence empowers no one. The humble takes his/her gifts to places where they are needed. Uses those talents where they can be multiplied. That's goes for the secular as well as the spiritual. Beside that, to make other fallible persons rich via the collection plate, borders on insanity.

Most of us agree wholeheartedly that there is work to be done. The one thing we all can agree on also, is that not many are going to do that work. When we know there's a need to be addressed, we've been conditioned in America to pray on it. Leave it there, so the old hymnal goes:

> Leave it there, leave it there,
> Take your burden to the Lord and leave it there.
> If you trust and never doubt,
> He will surely bring you out.
> Take your burden to the Lord and leave it there.

I am of the mind that we are equipped by an all-knowing God to make the desires of our hearts come to fruition. We must effect the change that we know is possible. We are the vehicles for making the impossible possible. More to the point, you can't wait on God to do what you can do for yourself.

Many have chided and some have even abandoned me for that position. That is okay now, and was okay then. It's better to know who the soldiers are. It is too easy to place everything on God: "God wanted it that way" or "I'm just waiting on God to answer." That is not to say that we shouldn't. But for those of us who are true believers (this chapter's for you), then we ought always have our eyes open to the many possibilities that God has placed before us. Don't blame God when you act or are inactive. If you believe that God has given man "free will", then you can't be blaming God for what you choose—or refuse—to do.

Spiritual Re-examination

Change does not roll in on the wheels of inevitability, but comes through continuous struggle. And so we must straighten our backs and work for our freedom. A man can't ride you unless your back is bent.

Have we not come to such an impasse in the modern world that we must love our enemies - or else? The chain reaction of evil - hate begetting hate, wars producing more wars - must be broken, or else we shall be plunged into the dark abyss of annihilation.

The bogus U. S. House of Representatives passed a non-binding resolution reaffirming "In God We Trust" as the national motto in November 2011. Nevermind the U.S., purportedly a Godly nation, had just finished up bombing human beings in Afghanistan, Libya and Pakistan. The United States stood by and allowed the Georgia execution of Troy Davis just the month before while reasonable doubt existed.

The measure sponsored by Rep. Randy Forbes, R-Va., supported and encouraged the motto's display in all public schools and government buildings. It was approved 396-9, with 2 abstentions. Nevermind the U.S. Constitution calls for a separation between church and state.

Keep in mind, this same body of Congress declined to pass legislation proposed by President Obama to provide jobs for Americans. Forbes said the resolution was needed because President Obama had once called "E pluribus unum" the national motto, and the Latin phrase meaning "from many one" was engraved in the new Capitol Visitors Center until Congress ordered that it be corrected. Was that "from many one" too much like diversity, or even unity?

Whatever the case, it was totally unnecessary and meant to hurt Obama and score points with the Religious Right. Rep. Jerrold Nadler, D-N.Y., called the resolution a meaningless distraction from the nation's real problems. "Nobody is threatening the national motto," he said.

This was an example how fake Christianity is proffered anytime white males feel threatened and powerless. With unemployment at 9% and the jobs bill looming, why is this even relevant to solving America's greater problems? Passing this resolution was designed to assert the old American trump card: if it's for God, then it's got to be right.

"In God We Trust" first appeared on U.S. coins during the Civil War in 1864. War is where nations—even divided ones—justify killing by claiming that "God is on our side," even though God supposedly prohibits murdering people. It officially became the national motto in 1956 and began appearing on paper currency the following year. More importantly, with or without the resolution, the motto is still the motto.

The piety of religion and religious people more often than not obstructs justice and just solutions to societal problems. Though God is thought to be a God of justice, Americans—especially the Evangelical Christians—follow those principles and precepts only when it's convenient. This contradiction causes others to doubt, disbelieve and even resist the calls of "godly conduct."

America has taught it's citizenry that "men are created equal," in particular, under the law. The law of the land dictates that men are equal in America. Yet, we fail to reconcile why an Equal Rights Amendment for women is not even a discussion in a "godly nation" such as this.

Once this law is established, in whatever form it exists, people are expected to follow it. If they fail to, measures are taken to punish the offenders. This punishment may involve physical pain, imprisonment, or some attack on the offenders' wellbeing, such as a monetary fine. In western society, the most common punishments are fines and imprisonment.

The Bible contains many examples of punishment for law-breaking. One dramatic example is in Hebrews:

> Hebrews 10:30: For we know Him who said, "Vengeance is Mine, I will repay," says the Lord. And again, "The LORD will judge His people." 31. It is a fearful thing to fall into the hands of the living God. (NKJV)

But what does that have to do with man executing punishment? When man does so, does this imply that man is God? If so, you begin to understand why you have such a struggle in an American society.
The idea that we would wait for God to answer our ills is welcomed by those who control societies of people—particularly, poor people. A good example is the Family Research Council. The Family Research Council (FRC) is a conservative or right-wing Christian group and lobbying organization formed in the United States in 1981 by James Dobson. In 1988, following financial difficulties, the FRC was incorporated into Focus on the Family. Tony Perkins joined the FRC as its president in 2003. Their political sway is rooted in religion. They use guilt in the form of "family values" to persuade Americans to subscribe to their ideology.

The claim is that if you don't subscribe to their brand of Christianity, then you lack "family values"—and are unworthy of being, not only an American, but a child of God. Who wants that designation?

The irony is that the leadership of the Family Research Council are a bunch of hypocrites who lack "family values." Not to mention that we must be acutely aware of who determines what "family values are! If those who make that determination can hold you in a condition of guilt, then they can persuade you to follow a direction that might redeem yourself...their direction.

Let me give you a good example: Joe Conason recently examined the religious right. Tony Perkins presented Rep. Joe Walsh, R-Ill. with the "True Blue" award, recognizing the legislator's "unwavering support of the family."

What's ironic about this bogus award is that Walsh, whose ex-wife is suing the freshman Congressman for failing to pay more than $100,000 in support owed for their three children. He claims that she agreed "verbally" that he could withhold payment whenever he was short of funds. Why would he be short on funds? He's a congressman not a retail clerk! She says he is lying. Either way, this distasteful dispute hardly reflects Walsh's deep devotion to family values.

But that's not unusual for these social controllers. The Walsh case is only the latest example of false piety. In that vein, Perkins may never surpass the Family Research Council's endorsement of Senator David Vitter (R-LA) last year – not long after the Louisiana Republican admitted to patronizing the notorious "D.C. Madam." At the time, Perkins scolded Vitter for adultery, while nevertheless praising him for his renewed commitment to their shared ideology.

These opponents of your equality in this society don't care about contradictory god-men, as long as they adhere to the extreme political positions of the religious right, which demand the repeal of health care reform, the revival of official discrimination against gays and lesbians, and the restriction of women's reproductive rights. That makes them defenders of "faith, family, and freedom," no matter what they may do to their kids.

We know of their unblushing fraudulence, which stretches back well over a decade to the years when Newt Gingrich and the Christian Coalition dominated Capitol Hill. Back then, vice of every variety ruined the marriages of many leading members of the Congressional class of 1994. But their personal behavior mattered not at all so long as they voted the corporate party line and recited the same old bigotries. These are people—"God-fearing" people— who have no concern to matters that benefit you.

They rail against Medicare and health care reform, which save families from devastation by rising insurance costs, unaffordable care, and pre-existing conditions. They oppose extending unemployment insurance, which permits jobless breadwinners to feed and shelter their families. They want to destroy Social Security, which permits the elderly to live with a modicum of dignity even when their families cannot afford to support them. They use religion to rope you in: if it's "of God," then it can't be wrong!

There are those who claim to espouse equal rights among the society, but act the role of God. In matters of employment, military, judiciary, environment, business and education, this mentality has proven detrimental to whomever falls into the underclass. It's usually people of color. God is the cover that serves as the justifier.

I'm not advising that you forsake God. I am encouraging you to redefine the way you were taught to relate with God as you are growing to understand him/her/it. You cannot allow fear to keep you in a submissive social position. That's what religion does and is designed to do in Western societies. Like sports, religion is a social control mechanism.

Social Control Theory

Social Control Theory proposes that people's relationships, commitments, values, norms, and beliefs encourage them not to break the laws of man. Thus, if moral codes are internalized and individuals are tied into, and have a stake in their wider community, they will voluntarily limit their propensity to commit deviant acts—as defined by those in control.

The theory seeks to understand the ways in which it is possible to reduce the likelihood of criminality (or adversarial acts and behaviors) developing in individuals. It does not consider motivational issues, simply stating that human beings may choose to engage in a wide range of activities, unless the range is limited by the processes of socialization and social learning.

In other words, religion is placed on a pedestal as infallible and unerring, thus it is never wrong and cannot be questioned. We are taught this in childhood and socialized into the belief system that it is unquestionably correct. Greater society introduces us into adulthood: autonomy (doing what's best for you), individualism (having to fend for yourself) and adventurism (exercising courage to take risks). In partaking in the natural progression of adulthood, we learn that all that was taught as right is always viable. Some of the boundaries are too restrictive to garner success.

We eventually test the boundaries and find that they are elastic. Depending on your societal status, one discovers how elastic those boundaries are. God has been used to keep the boundaries of people of color rigid. The dominant class uses rigid boundaries (more commonly known as laws) to keep the lower classes in submissive positions.

In early western civilization, priests and rulers both held enormous power, and were, in some respects almost interchangeable, given that they both wanted the same thing: a respectful, law-abiding, controlled populace, dedicated through a belief system that maintained the status quo, effectively, where the privileged used a combination of religion and politics (though to a lesser extent) to retain their status.

When looking through the world's major religions, many examples of attempts at social control can be seen. In Christianity, the Ten Commandments and the teachings of the Apostle Paul can be viewed as attempts to control through fear i.e. fear of divine retribution should an individual err into "godlessness". In Islam, the al'quran provides a framework and rules for daily living, and how an individual should behave, in almost every respect. Again, I'm not advocating the throwing out the baby with the bathwater, but the re-definition of your belief system and the methodology of its execution. It hasn't served you well.

There is an active war on you today as it was when Christopher Columbus first encountered the Americas. As devout orthodox Catholics, amassing wealth and dominating the Arawaks he encountered, came to be positively valued as a vital means of winning esteem among men and salvation of God in the afterlife. In a 1503 letter to the king and queen of Spain, Columbus said, "Gold is most excellent; gold constitutes treasure, and he who has it does all he wants in the world, and can even lift souls up to paradise." By

1493, Columbus planned to plunder Haiti—in the name of God.

For people of color, the God thing hasn't served us well. It surely has served and continues to serve as a means of solace in times of utter powerlessness, yet the oppressor has used religion as a guilt mechanism, a conformity tool and a justifier of contradiction.

The dominant control group would rather you wait on God to set you free from your oppressive condition. For those of us who grew up in church (not me), we know that God used Moses to set the Hebrew slaves bound in Egypt free. I say to you, that if the people did not rebel and say, "enough is enough" and get up and walk—despite the pursuit of Pharaoh and his army, they'd probably been in slavery another 2,000 years. History would've been drastically re-written.

Same deal today; you must do your praying...and then "put feet on your faith!"

Chapter Eight

As A Condition of Your Freedom, You Cannot...
Talk It to Death

"People may doubt what you say, but they will believe what you do."

~Lewis Cass

The power of speech has been greatly diminished by the foes of freedom, equality, justice and true democracy. I've always said that "if an almighty God could speak this world into existence, then words have some significance." During eras of societal change in America, men and woman have greased the wheels of disempowered constituencies of people with stirring words. Unfortunately, most of those words ended at the hearers ears.

Then, there are those who moved people to act. For a period of time, I had doubts about my effectiveness as an organizer at my height in Knoxville, Tennessee in the early 2000's. My doubts were allayed after I studied the life, work and assassination of Fred Hampton.

Fred Hampton was a young revolutionary that spoke harshly, yet accurately about his foes and honestly to his people. Hampton was a Black activist and deputy chairman of the Illinois chapter of the Black Panther Party (BPP). As a 21-year old, he was assassinated in 1969 as he lay in bed in his apartment by a tactical unit of the Cook County, Illinois State's Attorney's Office, in conjunction with the Chicago Police

Department and the Federal Bureau of Investigation (FBI).His rhetoric and work scared the hell out of the white political establishment. His effectiveness was the threat. He could only be effective if the people responded. It was time.

I examined my prosecution by the United States government and realized that my effectiveness facilitated my arrest, prosecution and conviction. (My effectiveness also facilitated my eventual appeal, overturn of that conviction and eventual release from imprisonment). Much like the case of Fred Hampton, the ability to voice the people's grievances and vision culminated into a threat to the establishment. That effectiveness is measured by end results. In the case of Hampton, assassination; in my case, arrest, prosecution and incarceration.

Leaders like Frederick Douglass, Geronimo Pratt, H. Rap Brown (aka Jamil al-Amin), Fred Hampton, Malcolm X and Stokely Carmichael moved people to the point of action. Words alone, only win a partial battle. The speaker must be willing to sacrifice and lead—even when the ones behind fall off.

One of the major fallacies within the struggle toward redemption and inclusion in a society filled with contradictions regarding class and race, is the perception that whites understand this struggle. Nothing can be farther than the truth. It is conceivable and realistic that they may understand the class struggle. Their history may contain ancestors who might've been Appalachian dwellers, union members, factory workers or immigrants from Europe. None of those groups are Negroid.

Stories have been written about bi-racial whites who "passed" for white knowing the experience. What we know about that is that they chose to stay on the white side of the track. They had a *choice*. In contrast, Blacks have not that choice.

Then there is the issue of white liberal anti-racists, like a Tim Wise, who eloquently speak against the ills of American racism. In an examination of poet and activist Ewuare Xola Osayande, "With the rise of Whiteness Studies on college campuses across the country has come the resurgence of whites as so-called experts on all matters pertaining to race. Among the most popular of them is the anti-racist speaker Tim Wise, who has become a regular presence on the college lecture circuit as well as in the media in the past few years. He has even been deemed the leader of the anti-racist movement by some of these very media outlets."

I see Tim Wise more often on CNN speaking many truths about white privilege and the curse of racism on America. Many blacks laud his straightforwardness and acuteness in addressing the role of whites in the injustices of race in America. What's faulty is that we give minds like Wise more credibility on the issue than the very people who experience it. This is a problematic proposition.

In 1841, the great orator, Frederick Douglass said:

> *"My friends, i have come to tell you something about slavery – what i know of it, as i have felt it. When i came north, i was astonished to find that the abolitionists knew so much about it, that they were acquainted with its effects as well as if they had lived in its midst. But though they can give you its history – though they can depict its horrors, they cannot speak as i can from experience ..."*

I'm crazy about the Pulitzer Prize-winning author of "Slavery by Another Name,"[22] Douglas Blackmon. I met him in 2010 and interviewed him on my radio show, socially speaking. His book was the disturbing account of a sordid chapter in American history—the lease (essentially the sale) of convicts to commercial interests between the end of the 19th century and well into the 20th. Usually, the criminal offense was loosely defined vagrancy or even changing employers without permission. The initial sentence was brutal enough; the actual penalty, reserved almost exclusively for black men, was a form of slavery in one of hundreds of forced labor camps operated by state and county governments, large corporations, small time entrepreneurs and provincial farmers.

Though Blackmon tells this story accurately, he cannot understand its significance in the lives of those people or those people's descendants, who, even today, are affected by this injustice. The Rev. Martin Luther King said, "Discrimination is a hellhound that gnaws at Negroes in every waking moment of their lives to remind them that the lie of their inferiority is accepted as truth in the society dominating them." Whites have not that worry...and never will.

Let me tell you about Henrietta Lacks. Her story is a good example of how whites are more often than not, the teller of our stories. Journalist Rebecca Skloot reportedly tracked down the story—that was a secret.[23] I have to inform you, the reader, that Blacks have a more difficult time telling our story, because the holder of the combination to the vault are white people. We are not afforded access to the vault, much less, the combination.

Henrietta Lacks was a black tobacco farmer from southern Virginia who got cervical cancer when she was 30. A doctor at Johns Hopkins took a piece of her tumor without telling her and sent it down the hall to scientists there who had been trying to grow tissues in culture for decades without success. No one knows why, but her cells never died.

Henrietta's cells were the first immortal human cells ever grown in culture. They were essential to developing the polio vaccine. They went up in the first space missions to see what would happen to cells in zero gravity. Many scientific landmarks since then have used her cells, including cloning, gene mapping and in vitro fertilization. But do you think Mrs. Lacks received a dime for this contribution to society?

In 1951, a scientist at Johns Hopkins Hospital in Baltimore, Maryland, created the first immortal human cell line with a tissue sample taken from a young black woman with cervical cancer. Those cells, called HeLa cells, quickly became invaluable to medical research— though their donor remained a mystery for decades. It's simple: the evidence speaks for itself. America has robbed it's more vulnerable. No other way to say it; you can't talk it to death.

I went to an affordable housing seminar in 2011 held by a very effective non-profit group in DC. The group attempted to educate the participants of the history of

Washington, DC, in particular the historically black section of southeast DC called Anacostia.

The name "Anacostia" comes from the anglocized name of a Nacochtank Native Americans settlement along the AnacostiaRiver. The core of what is now the Anacostia historic district was incorporated in 1854 as Uniontown and was one of the first suburbs in the District of Columbia.

It was designed to be financially available to Washington's working class, many of whom were employed across the river at the Navy Yard; its (then) location outside of and isolated from the city made its real estate inexpensive. The initial subdivision of 1854 carried restrictive covenants prohibiting the sale, rental or lease of property to anyone of African or Irish descent. Abolitionist Frederick Douglass, often called "the sage of Anacostia," bought Cedar Hill, the estate belonging to the developer of Uniontown, in 1877 and lived there until he died in 1895. The home is still maintained as a historical site in Anacostia. Blacks in DC know this.

During the Civil War, Anacostia was protected by a series of forts upon the hills southwest of the city. Following the conclusion of the war, the forts were dismantled and the land returned to its original owners.

Anacostia's population remained predominantly European-American up until the late 1950s and early 1960's, with Whites comprising 87% of the population. During the 1960s, the Anacostia Freeway (I-295) was constructed. The highway imposed a barrier between the Anacostia neighborhood and the Anacostia River waterfront. This was intentional.

Numerous public housing apartment complexes were also built in the neighborhood. With the flight of much of the middle class out of the neighborhood during the late 1950s and 1960's with the opportunity to move to newer housing in postwar suburbs, Anacostia's demographics changed dramatically as the neighborhood became predominantly African American. Later events with the rise of drugs and poverty adversely affected the area as it gained an infamous reputation.

After the gentrification boom of the late 2000's, whites took authority over Anacostia as if they'd been there all along. As of the 2000 Census, Anacostia's population was 92% Black-American, 5% Non-Hispanic White, and 3% other. By 2010, the population of D.C. was just over 50% Black, 38.5% White, 19% Hispanic, 3.5% Asian, and 0.3% Native American. Individuals from other races made up 4.1% of the District's population according to the Census. Although the bean counters said that Black numbers were still above 90%, Anacostia is looking more and more like Europe.

So back to the seminar...a white male, under 30 years old, was chosen to serve as the curator of the seminar—effectively telling us the story of our own community! Of course I was upset and offended that something such as this could even be presented to a group of Black people, but most of the participants were women, and unfortunately those who lack knowledge of our history.

I was pissed because we have well-known historians who walk among us like Professor C.R. Gibbs. My question is why wouldn't this non-profit seek out Blacks to tell the story of Blacks. The answer is, because as gentrifiers, they don't want Blacks to be the authority on anything that whites will run.

Yet, in America, we rely on the scholarship of whites to tell our story. Their word is accepted as the final authority on any subject, and even worse, any subject concerning blacks. Just turn your radio dial to National Public Radio. Those whites speak unashamed and authoritative on issues of Black import. My listening and financial support of NPR is evaporated to nil after making an exhaustive study of their broadcasting.

If they were accurate, then maybe my admonition would be different, but their reports concerning blacks and minorities are from the eyes of whites. Whites are painted as "saviors" and all else are dependents. This is not an accident. Traditionalists sat and thought up the language and visualizations the implant in the minds of everyday Americans—black and white—to subscribe to this theory. Very unhealthy for a real America.

It only makes sense that we not defer our experience over to people who can never—and will never—go to the john brown level for the cause. In community organizing, whites often offer themselves as allies in issues of black import, and subsequently end up running the agenda. This is unacceptable. What is acceptable is that they come alongside us and walk in lockstep. Serving as advisors and consultants and even sounding boards is an acceptable role for whites who believe in the wrongs committed and being committed by this nation.

More to the point, we can't get caught up in eloquent orators—though they may be committed, sincere and dedicated to a cause—who aren't willing to lose some skin in battle for justice. More often than not, they will tell you, as intellectuals, that they will "fight for you, pray for you, but won't pick up a brick." My point here is simple: Don't talk it to death. Writing a book does not change legislation. Giving a speech does not foster an investigation (though whistle-blowing might). Having warm bodies with feet on the street—in the faces of decision-makers—is among the only things that brings change in America. The other thing is violence, but that's chapter ten.

Now, I'm not saying that we are not to speak our story, our opinion, our vision or our intent at each best opportunity; what I am saying is that we should be wise and effective in doing so. We cannot fail to take painstaking efforts to be accurate, relevant and timely.

One of the surest ways to lose momentum—and your human resources—is to talk, talk and talk. That formula is a proven loser. Talk, plan and act is a much more effective formula for moving the mountains of injustice.

Chapter Nine

As A Condition of Your Freedom, You Cannot...
Apologize

"The only correct actions are those that demand no explanation and no apology."

~Red Auerbach

I know that my life hit the glass ceiling for several reasons. Some of my navigation issues are solely attributed to the "creative design" by others. I got myself into trouble with the law during the early 1990's. No excuses to be made. With work hard to obtain, I found it necessary to earn income—and did.

Between drugs and petty crimes, I found viable activities to create income for my personal purpose to exist. Unfortunately for me, like many young Black men, the world of illegal acts only carry themselves temporarily, but creative design make the effects linger for life.

Do not apologize for being angry...you didn't design the system

A felony conviction in 1995 meant more to my life's stagnation that I could've ever known at the time. All I knew was that the government chose not to pursue me anymore on an allegation and offered me a plea deal. Three-and-a-half years of postponing hearings had wore on me, nevermind, I wasn't guilty of the crime charged. My view was, after all I *had* done, this was an acceptable trade-off. All I knew is I wouldn't have to come back to court. That's how my court-appointed attorney, Les Jeffers, sold the deal to me.

This is the profile for many of America's people of color. All they know is that they don't have to stay in jail another day or come back to court. Unwittingly and relieved, they accept a disability called Probation. It's a creative design that has crippled millions of Americans—in particular, people of color.

But that's not the point of this chapter...creative design is. Like many in America, had I the resources to hire an attorney, chances are 80% better that I would've avoided a conviction for the alleged charge against me. Creative design dictates that poor people, under-educated people and people of color shall always have a glass ceiling precipitated by legislation and societal "norms" imposed by those in power.

Creative design was overtly applied during the re-election campaign of Barack Obama. Race-neutral laws were drafted that created "disabilities" for people of color. If whites were affected, there were so few of the white population, they were considered collateral damage.

After the Republicans won the U.S. House of Representatives in 2010, voter suppression laws appeared on state agendas. States across the country passed a wave of laws that could've made it harder to vote. The Brennan Center chronicled these laws in their Voting Law Changes in 2012 report.[24] Overall, 25 laws and two executive actions passed in 19 states since the beginning of 2011. Though race-neutral, there laws adversely intentionally affected people of color.

In September of 2012, *The Christian Science Monitor* forecasted that the newly passed voter I.D. laws could've affected 10 million Hispanic voters.[25]Republicans knew that their racist rhetoric and adverse policies towards Hispanics put them at risk of losing that constituency, but still perpetrated the illusion that they would win the Hispanic vote. They calculated that voter I.D. laws would suppress their votes. President Obama carried 69% of the Hispanic vote.

"Creative design" was met with stark opposition from groups like the NAACP, the ACLU, among other voting rights advocacies. Citizens rejected these laws at the polls, nearly a dozen courts overturned or weakened restrictive measures, and the Department of Justice blocked others. You must refuse to apologize when racists retard the rules.

Allow me to expound using the research of Michelle Alexander: If you take into account prisoners, a large majority of African American men in some urban areas, like Chicago, Philadelphia, Washington, DC, have been labeled felons for life.

These men are part of a growing undercaste—not class, CASTE—a group of people who are permanently relegated, by law, to an inferior second-class status. They can be denied the right to vote, automatically excluded from juries, and legally discriminated against in employment, housing, access to education, and public benefits -- much as their grandparents and great-grandparents once were during the Jim Crow era. Jim Crow was creative design; i.e., white males cunningly designed a system to keep a certain class if people in the underclass with no prospect of upward mobility—no matter how hard or talented one might be.

In other words, it's not your inabilities to negotiate the system that holds you in an inferior social position, it's the creators of the navigation methods who "creatively designed" the system that placed you—and keep you there. One cannot "pull himself up by his bootstraps" when the boots were made without straps.

On October 23, 2011, CBS News' 60 Minutes highlighted the late Apple CEO/co-founder Steve Jobs. All of his genius, all of his brilliance...all of the abrasive aspects of his character, were not prohibitive to his success. Those same character flaws are exactly what whites use to deny Blacks access to the avenues of success in America. Being "mean and petulant" are diametrically opposite of good character, but Jobs (through adoption) was raised in a 1950's community of engineers...no Blacks there. Clearly advantageous; I want you to Google it and watch it.

You'll see how perspective can make you goat or hero; valiant or villain...once you see it, you'll realize why the rich get no props from me. They work no harder, they are no smarter than anyone else; like author Malcolm Gladwell exposes in his bestselling book, they are "*Outliers*": beneficiaries of favorable circumstances...period.

Being white and privileged in America will have you avoid prison, poverty and mental anguish; you might not avoid hell, but you will live well. You have nothing to apologize to American society for; it owes you. If you're reading this book, then chances are you have not been the beneficiary of "favorable" circumstances. If you grew up poor, you likely didn't know it until somebody told you that you were. When you became an adult, you knew that you struggled and that there were others who didn't. You probably spent a portion of your life trying to figure out why? I'm here to tell you that it wasn't your fault. It was all part of a greater man-made design.

I watched the July 2011 House of Representatives hearing on Sen. Harry Reid's Debt Ceiling plan. It was the hot political topic of the summer. The Republicans rejected it—because they didn't get what they wanted. They wanted to cut government spending on the very programmatic expenditures that support and allow navigation of the system by the majority of American people—poor people. More cuts to Medicare and Medicaid; cuts to education funding for under-privileged college students. The Republicans wanted to protect the profits of corporations, investment income of high-income earners. This is why you don't have to apologize.

During the election of 2012, republican candidate Mitt Romney was exposed when remarks he made, secretly recorded during a fundraiser in May and posted online in September by the magazine _Mother Jones_, showed how privileged white males truly regard the rest of Americans—which is populated with Black and brown people. Specifically, he said, "There are 47 percent who are with [Obama], who are dependent upon government, who believe that they are victims, who believe that government has a responsibility to care for them, who believe that they are entitled to health care, to food, to housing, to you name it."

"Forty-seven percent of Americans pay no income tax," Romney said, and that his role "is not to worry about those people. I'll never convince them they should take personal responsibility and care for their lives."

You see, there are a band of Americans—particularly, Republicans—who want you to fail. These people are the ones who have creatively designed the system in a way that keeps you—as a formerly convicted person, for one—from getting your life back. Once you are released from prison, not only is your time not complete, but you are forever subject to legalized discrimination by potential employers and/or those who might contract for your services. You are in that 47%.

Apologize for A History You Didn't Create?

What I speak of at every opportunity is the way our American system hoodwinks us into thinking and believing that our country comes from a history of morality, fairness and democracy for all of its inhabitants. Such a sham...then reminders resurface like Columbus' "discovery" of America, Wilmington 1898, Tulsa 1921 or the Marines at Montford Point.

To the latter instance, in June, 1941, President Franklin D. Roosevelt issued an order that began to erase discrimination in the armed forces. Why did it exist in the first place if this country was so hellbent on democracy and justice? The Marines were the last to open up and the next year, 18,000 young black men trained -- not at Parris Island -- but at a *segregated* facility in Montford Point, North Carolina.

Montford Point Marines were fighting the war on racism and Jim Crow and at the same time they were getting ready to fight a war overseas. These history-making Marines never received the same recognition as the famed Tuskegee Airmen, Black pilots who fought in World War II. But the few Montford Marines who are still alive reunite each year at their convention and hope to spread the word about the path they paved. But most of us have never heard about them. That's part of creative design.

To preserve their legacy, they are supporting a bill that would grant Congressional Gold Medals for the first black Marines. In 2012, Commandant Gen. James Amos met with the Montford Point survivors and presided over a month-long effort to pay tribute to them. It took 70 years...

Though we know how times have changed, the glass ceiling that existed—by creative design—caused these men a life of hardship and loss of potential income that intentionally kept them from realizing the American Dream. It is unreasonable for these men to apologize for failing to rise the highest echelon of American society like we of today are expected to do. These marines were born into a cunningly and creatively designed system that prevented them from reaching the ideal American existence, a predecessor of today's Black man.

For Edwin Fizer, a surviving marine from Montford Point, he found it important to be among others who can understand the sting of discrimination while choosing to serve the nation. You see, sadly not every marine, much less, every American will understand— or even more, respect—that struggle.

"They treated us poorly. We heard the 'n' word a lot," Fizer said. It was an experiment of sorts to see whether black men had enough steeliness to fight as a Marine, he said. That's an example of the graciousness of Black people...even, willful ignorance. I contend that whites were secondarily concerned about whether or not Black men had the guts to be Marines, but simply set up barriers to ensure their failure (like the Republicans did to Barack Obama during his term as president). Their weapons and equipment were inferior and the tests of physical fitness, twice as difficult.

If a drill called for a 10-mile run, the black recruits were ordered to run 20. This is an example of glass ceiling design. Policy and institutional rules are contrived so that Blacks (and people of color) will fail. Whites rarely have those barriers to overcome, especially when they are the ones who make the policies.

I know what that design looks like as I was a soldier in the early 1980's and faced that same policy construction at my first duty station at Fort Campbell, Kentucky. To this day, this design has negatively affected the path and trajectory of my life from that point forward. The benign nature of this contortion of policy only causes societal interactionaries to blame me for the lack of rise in my quest for the American Dream. I know who corrupted my path and I owe no apology for pin-pointing the tactics or the culprits.

Do not apologize for seeking reparations

One thing I have to tell you America—both Black and white—is that America owes Black people...and I'm not talking about an apology either. The fact that Black men have not prospered to the degree of whites is in no way the fault of Black men...to the contrary, white men are to blame, if that is a necessary course of discussion. It shouldn't even *have* to be discussed, because we all *know* that.

You may know the story of the eugenics victims of North Carolina. Under the guise of weeding out "imbeciles" and criminals, many states sterilized minorities and the poor, not telling the victims what was actually happening. Indiana passed the first state Eugenics bill in 1907, and 32 states ended up passing eugenics laws (Nevada and New Jersey had eugenics laws that were not formally acted upon). Good ol' U.S. of A.

This was wrong beyond all comprehension, but suffice it to say, around 60,000 people were sterilized across America. The program ran from 1909 through 1977, peaking in the 1950s. The program continued beyond the 1948 U.N. Universal Declaration of Human Rights. America practiced eugenics for almost 70 years. The victims sought compensation from our government. People who are wronged by our government generally do that.

On virtually the same day in January of 2012, two groups of people in America who were wronged received compensation for their suffering. One group was white, another was predominantly black.

Virginia-based Alpha Natural Resources (who bought the offending company, Massey Energy) settled wrongful death lawsuits with families of all 29 victims of West Virginia's Upper Big Branch coal mine explosion of April 2010. Just weeks after the blast, Massey offered $3 million to each family. It didn't take years! Some accepted, but most refused, saying the lives of their loved ones had no price tags. I'd agree. But in January of 2012, the word was each family received at least $3 million. This group was white.

On the same day, it was announced that North Carolina had become the first U.S. state to offer compensation to survivors of its eugenics program. 72 such survivors had been located at the time. North Carolina offered each of them between $20,000 and $50,000 as a "sorry we tried to wipe out your family" payout. This is 5% of the $1,000,000 originally sought. This group was Black...not all eugenics victims were Black, but you know who took the brunt of this intentional inhumane act.

Okay, in this picture, if you are black, you get $50,000 for your troubles; if you're white, you receive $3million. What's wrong with this picture? And Republicans in congress passed Tort Reform because they told us that "people are greedy?" Is this an instance when you'd be sorry to be Black? It wasn't the fault of the eugenics *victims* that somebody chose to ruin their lives, but they had to pay a hefty price. These Blacks are made to feel guilty for bringing up race in not only the offense against them, but the resulting remedy. Why are you complaining?

Not Enough Money to Go Around...

When the most recent recession hit this country, pundits and economists postured as if to search for reason for the country's economic crisis (started during the Bush administration). We, as Black men, already knew the reasons:

1. white men stole all the money
2. white men stole all the money, and
3. white men stole all the money

Whenever there is a recession in America, it's because white men steal all the money, then stow it away in off-shore banks and wait patiently for bail outs and tough austerity measures, then they show up rich. They get credit from the presiding administration for being "bold investors" with *their* money (repatriating that which they stole), saving the American economy.

Of course, here, I indict America, but this is a worldwide practice that afflicts poor whites too. Cabals of white men (and you can name a few Black ones too!) steal from nations big and small, capitalist and socialist alike, and poor people pay the price. National leaders portray themselves as "bold" or "daring" when they execute austerity measures to right their respective economies.

Heck, in January 2012, three Swiss bankers had been charged with helping American taxpayers hide more than $1.2 billion from the Internal Revenue Service. Michael Berlinka, UrsFrei and Roger Keller faced up to five years in prison for their roles in the scheme. They were accused of helping more than 100 clients hide assets between 2005 and 2010.

The indictment identified the defendants' place of employment only as the Zurich branch of "Swiss Bank A," though accounts in the names of Berlinka and Keller appeared on the professional networking site Xing.com with Wegelin & Co., a bank in Switzerland, listed as their employer. You *know* what I'm going to say next?

They play the mainstream media game—with politicians and economists as deflectors—while poor, working class people get their heads knocked off. Unions are downsized, teachers are maligned and fired, public works (including public schools) are privatized just a little more each recession. In the words of the late George Carlin, "it's all bullshit."

But it's more than that. Real people's lives are decimated in the process while unseen thieves make off with a nation's wealth. Let me give you a good example: In December of 2011, Jon Corzine, the former CEO of bankrupt broker-dealer MF Global (MFG)—not to mention a former New Jersey governor and U.S. senator—said that he did not know the whereabouts of the company's missing customer funds, according to testimony in front of the House Agriculture Committee.

The company's financial situation turned sour due to its large **bets** (with *other people's money*) on the European sovereign debt, and when the European crisis intensified, it became one of the largest bankruptcies in corporate history.

"I simply do not know where the money is, or why the accounts have not been reconciled to date," Corzine announced in his prepared statement, although he did apologize to shareholders, customers, and employees. In real time, apologies are worth what?

Experts at the committee hearing estimated that as much as $1.2 **billion** of customer funds could've been missing. The Agriculture Committee had oversight of the Commodities Futures Trading Commission (CFTC), a regulator of MFG. Though they have oversight, there ain't a white male going to jail for this theft. And to think, conservative Republicans fight tooth-to-nail *against* regulation of this industry...and we're none the wiser.

I can't leave out the example of Russell Wasendorf, Sr., Chairman of PFGBest, who tried to kill himself in July of 2012 after being exposed for stealing the money.

In a Bernie Madoff-like scam, Wasendorf prepared bank statements that appeared to make the firm look strong, stating that they had $200million when they really had $5million. According to prosecutors, he was skimming money from his customer accounts, to the tune of more than $100 million. Unemployment was at 8% during most of 2012. Companies don't hire once money is pilfered and governments bail companies out.

I have to bring to your remembrance the case of Aubrey Lee price.47-year-old "Lee" Price -- whom the

FBI characterized as an investment adviser and former minister -- had to be captured to get "the people's" money.

In late 2010, Price was being celebrated by his peers and written up in newspaper articles after a company that he controlled bought a controlling portion of the troubled Montgomery Bank & Trust in Ailey, which is located some 170 miles southeast of Atlanta.

He was supposed to invest the bank's capital. Instead, Price used a New York-based "clearing firm" -- a dummy company set up to hide money -- to cover up fraudulent wire transfers and investments. Price and others "raised approximately $40 million from approximately 115 investors," mostly in Georgia and Florida, beginning in 2009, then instead of investing the money as promised, Price fraudulently wired the bank's funds to accounts that he personally controlled at other financial institutions and provided bank management with altered documents to make it appear as if he had invested the bank's money in (U.S.) Treasury securities."

In sum, Price hid the embezzlement by falsely stating that about $17 million had been deposited in the bank's name at a New York financial services firm.

By the time these charges came out, Price had been missing for several weeks, having told friends he had lost "a large sum of money through his trading activities." In the letter he'd purportedly written to acquaintances and business associates, Price indicated that he planned to kill himself by "jumping off a ferry boat" off Florida's coast.

He was spotted—alive—in Key West, Florida, in the middle of that month, and the U.S. Coast Guard's subsequent search for his body found nothing. He faked his death and was captured in late-December 2013, changed identity, growing marijuana, in Brunswick, Georgia...facing 30 years in prison.

This is where the money goes when conservative republicans argue for "less government regulations," lower taxes for "job creators" and "smaller government" (so there aren't enough personnel to catch these thieves). Recessions are caused by greedy, unscrupulous, cash thieves.

Now, I don't know where the 115 investors got their money or what else they were going to do with it, but I do know that $40 million could make the $40,000 annual salaries of 1,000 working-class families and individuals in this country. That amounts to jobs, consumer spending, a healthier American economy and a greater quality of life.

They Steal, We Suffer

In the meantime, the Black unemployment rate doubles that of whites, all the while Blacks are accused of not working hard enough to find work (the same claim by Republicans made against those Americans receiving unemployment insurance in early 2014), as the Latino immigration population work for less than acceptable wages. It's the divide and conquer scheme of Willie Lynch proportions. And what's funny about it all is that we've seen it all before. In the end, white men get rich.

So let me tell you why whites are better off in American society than Blacks. It's not because they work any harder or are any smarter. It's solely because they are greedier and a bit craftier in maintaining the lop-sided system that their forefathers put in place. Each generation, they lose another step, but they were so far ahead 330 years ago that it's extremely difficult to make up such a huge head start.

Academians, Darrick Hamilton and William Darity, authors of a 2010 study of the wealth disparity gap, put it like this: Recessions disproportionately affect black and Latino families. During the 1999–2001 recession, median household wealth fell by 27% for both Latinos and Blacks, while it grew by 2% for whites. The current recession likely will worsen the racial wealth gap.

Although whites are more likely than blacks to own their home, the share of black wealth in the form of housing is nearly twice as large as the white share. And with blacks far more likely than whites to have been steered toward sub-prime loans in discriminatory credit markets, the foreclosure crisis is bound to have a more deleterious effect on black wealth than on white wealth.

For example, a recent report on mortgage lending and race by the Institute on Race and Poverty at the University of Minnesota found that black Twin City residents earning over $150,000, in comparison to whites earning below $40,000, were twice as likely to be denied a home loan. Those fortunate (or unfortunate) enough to get a loan were more than three times as likely to have a sub-prime loan.

White analysts, pundits and politicians like Newt Gingrich have consistently blamed Blacks for their home losses within the home foreclosure debacle in America. They have blamed Blacks for "buying houses they couldn't afford." This makes me distance myself from whites—any white person—though all whites don not subscribe to that theory. Any person observing that era in history cannot genuinely agree with that analysis. What's unfortunate in this country is that many—especially conservative supporters stand with the Gingriches of America...no matter how inaccurate the statement is.

The theory may be righteous, but the analysis is an outright lie. The U.S. Department of Justice reached settlements with Wells Fargo in July 2012, and Luther Burbank Savings in September of 2012 for discriminatory loan practices. In December of 2011, Bank of America agreed to pay $335 million to resolve allegations that its Countrywide unit engaged in a widespread pattern of discrimination against qualified Black-American and Hispanic borrowers on home loans. Since BOA didn't take ownership of Countrywide while they were discriminating against Black folks, they absolved themselves from the behavior. Of course, BOA had their own racist practices—in the banking sector.

At the time of this settlement, the DOJ said it was the largest settlement in history over residential fair lending practices. The settlement was only the tip of the iceberg. But this tip was a significant part of the destabilized American economy. This was not the fault of Black homeowners that they had to apologize for.

According to that DOJ complaint, Countrywide charged over 200,000 Black-American and Hispanic borrowers higher fees and interest rates than non-Hispanic white borrowers with a similar credit profile. But of course, our conservative analysts, pundits and politicians will not admit this isn't the fault of the borrowers. The complaint said that these borrowers were charged higher fees and rates because of their race or national origin rather than any other objective criteria.

The United States' complaint said that Countrywide was aware that the fees and interest rates that its loan officers (individuals) were charging discriminated against Black-American and Hispanic borrowers, but failed to impose meaningful limits or guidelines to stop it. This is why I distrust white Americans. These were individuals (albeit, doing the corporation's bidding) executing acts of racism. I don't have to apologize for being a victim of other people's hatred.

By steering borrowers into subprime loans from 2004 to 2007, the complaint alleged, Countrywide harmed those qualified Black-American and Hispanic borrowers. Don't they realize that when you hurt one sector of the American populace, you hurt the whole? Newt Gingrich nor Mitt Romney will admit that.

I recall how conservatives castigated under-water homeowners who were fleeced and re-fleeced under the Home Affordable Modification Program (HAMP). I read a blog at National Review on-line (my enemy) and a guy named Kevin D. Williamson helped me break down the home foreclosure theft. It was a fraud from Day One: It was designed to do nothing but camouflage the effects of the housing meltdown. It was based on bribery—paying the banks to modify (or pretend to consider modifying) mortgages that they really had no interest in modifying. But they took gladly took the money and put on a mime's face in the process.

My mother was a victim of HAMP—and so was her American Dream. Here's how it worked: Fannie Mae got paid an undisclosed amount of money to administer the program, and its payments were structured in such a way that it had an incentive to push more people through the application process (I helped my mother through hers). A former Fannie Mae insider charged in a whistle-blower lawsuit that Fannie's main concern in administering HAMP was maximizing its own fees.

The banks and "mortgage servicers" got paid to put people into modification trials, and their incentives were structured in such a way that if it makes sense to go ahead and foreclose anyway after the trial, then they made money doing that, too. But not until they extended the trial to whatever point maximizes their financial return.

But to get to the point of this chapter, the worst feature of HAMP wasn't that it wasted American money. Practically every penny spent was a waste, if not an active instance of economic destruction, but it had spent only about $1 billion of the many billions set aside for it. Where do you think the other billions went? (Oddly enough, in Washington, the chief complaint with HAMP was that it hadn't spent ENOUGH of the funds appropriated to it. That kind of thinking is how you get a $14 trillion federal debt.) The crime of HAMP is that it hosed the people it was allegedly set up to help: struggling homeowners...and Black homeowners got saddled with the blame of buying a home they couldn't afford. This era helped widen the wealth disparity gap.

Economic studies also demonstrate that inheritances, bequests, and intra-family transfers account for more of the racial wealth gap than any other demographic and socioeconomic factor, including education, income, and household structure. These intra-familial transfers, the primary source of wealth for most Americans with positive net worth, are transfers of blatant non-merit resources. Why do blacks have vastly fewer resources to leave to the next generation?

Apart from the national failure to endow ex-slaves with the promised "40 acres and a mule" after the Civil War, blacks were deprived systematically of property, especially land, accumulated between 1880 and 1910 by government complicity and fraud as well as seizures by white terrorists. During the first three decades of the 20th century, white rioters destroyed prosperous black communities from Wilmington, North Carolina, to Tulsa, Oklahoma. Restrictive covenants, redlining, general housing and lending discrimination also inhibited blacks from accumulating wealth.

A recent analysis gave this country a shot in the arm. According to an analysis of Census data by the Pew Research Center[26], cited by the AP, the median wealth — defined as assets minus debts — of white U.S. households in 2009 was $113,149, compared with

$6,325 for Hispanics and $5,677 for blacks. That doesn't even sound right saying, much less look right reading it!

The wealth gap between whites and minorities in the U.S. is the widest it's been in a quarter-century, with white households having 20 times the net worth of Hispanic and black households.

Even if a white American is unemployed, they can survive with less adverse consequences while seeking re-employment than those of any other race.

The wealth disparity—partly due to the fact that many whites derive their wealth from stocks and corporate savings, while minority families are mostly invested in their homes — was worsened by the housing bubble bursting and financial meltdown.

Hispanics were reportedly hardest hit by the recession — between 2005 and 2009, their median wealth fell more than 66 percent to just over $6,000, the research reportedly shows.

"What's pushing the wealth of whites is the rebound in the stock market and corporate savings, while younger Hispanics and Black-Americans who bought homes in the last decade — because that was the American dream — are seeing big declines," Timothy Smeeding, a University of Wisconsin-Madison professor who specializes in income inequality, told The Associated Press.

In case you missed it earlier, the white-black wealth gap is also the widest since the census began tracking such data in 1984, when the ratio was roughly 12 to 1.

Given the importance of intergenerational transfers of wealth and past and present barriers preventing black wealth accumulation, private action and market forces alone cannot close an unjust racial wealth gap—public-sector intervention is necessary.

Wealth disparity causes poverty

More than 1 in 7 Americans were living in poverty, not statistically different from the 46.2 million of 2011 and the sixth straight year the rate had failed to improve, the Census Bureau reported. Mississippi had the highest share of its residents in poverty, at 22 percent, according to rough calculations by the Census Bureau. It was followed by Louisiana, New Mexico and Arkansas. On the other end of the scale, New Hampshire had the lowest share, at 8.1 percent. It doesn't pay to be Black in the south.

Median income for the nation's households was $51,017, also unchanged from the previous year after two consecutive annual declines, while the share of people without health insurance did improve but only a bit, from 15.7 percent to 15.4 percent.

In other to solve the problem, you've got to seize the cause. The problem is poverty; the cause is wealth disparity. President Obama set a theme that stated he'd pursue in the final years of his presidency: growing income disparity in the U.S. is the "defining challenge or our time" and Washington must confront it.

Too bad his premise came five years into his presidency. I'm of the mind that President Obama should've ran progressive policy changes down the throat of Republicans from 2009 on. He might not have lived to see 2010, but neither did Kennedy...and the country benefitted greatly from the second-greatest social revolution in American history.

White males in congress—chiefly Republican lawmakers—made it priority to not allow that to happen. They'd enjoyed great success in making that gap as wide as it is beginning in the era of Ronald Regan. President Regan was the mouthpiece of "trickle down" economic policies that simply posited, if you make rich people richer, that money will trickle down on the lower classes. Lower taxes, less government regulation and corporate subsidies have only made the wealth gap wider, especially for Blacks—and increased poverty in America as a whole.

Do not apologize for being black

That sounds so very elementary, even insulting to think that anyone would consider it, but many do. Most, in the privacy of their breath, some to their children for bringing them into a society of imbalance, improbability and impossibility. What is factual is no one should ever apologize for being who they are.

But then, why would that even be an issue? It's an issue because America has partitioned cultural differences as the lines in the sands for war. As the conservative political commentator, Bill O'Reilly puts it, "culture war." According to the new encyclopedia, Wikipedia, the culture war is defined as a metaphor used to claim that socio-political conflict is based on sets of conflicting cultural values. The term frequently implies a conflict between those values considered traditionalist or conservative and those considered progressive or liberal. The "culture war" is sometimes traced to the 1960s and has taken various forms since then.

Historically speaking, as an American phenomenon, its origin was in the 1920s when urban and rural American values came into clear conflict. This followed several decades of immigration to the cities by elements considered alien by the earlier immigrants and was a result of the cultural shifts and modernizing trends of the Roaring 20's, culminating in the presidential campaign of Al Smith. The common element in then and now is *different*.

Anything different from what the ruling class—white people in America's case—deems as appropriate" is determined to be wrong. Whether music, entertainment choices, political organization or socialization, any difference in getting to the same result can be grounds for war—a culture war.

I've seen that war take definition and specific shape. The expression was introduced again by the 1991 publication of *Culture Wars: The Struggle to Define America*[27] by James Davison Hunter, a sociologist at the University of Virginia. In it, Hunter described what he saw as a dramatic realignment and polarization that had transformed American politics and culture. Let me translate: what that meant was the white man was losing power.

He argued that on an increasing number of "hot-button" defining issues — abortion, gun politics, separation of church and state, privacy, recreational drug use, homosexuality (or same-sex relationships), censorship issues — there had come to be two definable polarities.

Furthermore, it was not just that there were a number of divisive issues, but that society had divided along essentially the same lines on each of these issues, so as to constitute two warring groups, defined primarily not by nominal religion, ethnicity, social class, or even political affiliation, but rather by ideological world views, thus the liberal and conservative terminology of today.

Hunter characterized this polarity as stemming from opposite impulses, toward what he refers to as *Progressivism* and *Orthodoxy*. The dichotomy has been adopted with varying labels, including, for example, by the aforementioned Bill O'Reilly who emphasizes differences between "Secular-Progressives" and "Traditionalists". Of course, the terms are chosen by the attacker, that's why we should never trust their terms.

I recall as a young man when in 1990, commentator Pat Buchanan mounted a campaign for the Republican nomination for President against incumbent George H. W. Bush in 1992. He received a prime time speech slot at the 1992 Republican National Convention, which is sometimes dubbed the "**'culture war' speech.**"

During his speech, he said: "There is a religious war going on in our country for the soul of America. It is a cultural war, as critical to the kind of nation we will one day be as was the Cold War itself." In addition to criticizing "environmental extremists" and "radical feminism," he said public morality was a defining issue:

> The agenda [Bill] Clinton and [Hillary] Clinton would impose on America — abortion on demand, a litmus test for the Supreme Court, homosexual rights, discrimination against religious schools, women in combat — that's change, all right. But it is not the kind of change America wants. It is not the kind of change America needs. And it is not the kind of change we can tolerate in a nation that we still call God's country.

Buchanan received high acclaim and set the stage for the assault on poor people. A month later, Buchanan elaborated that this conflict was about power over society's definition of right and wrong. He named abortion, sexual orientation and popular culture as major fronts – and mentioned other controversies, including clashes over the Confederate Flag, Christmas and taxpayer-funded art. He also said that the negative attention his talk of a culture war received was itself evidence of America's polarization. Funny how attackers use the tactic of painting themselves as the victims….

When Buchanan ran for President in 1996, he promised to fight for the conservative side of the culture war:

> I will use the bully pulpit of the Presidency of the United States, to the full extent of my power and ability, to defend American traditions and the values of faith, family, and country, from any and all directions. And, together, we will chase the purveyors of sex and violence back beneath the rocks whence they came.

Who do you think he was talking about? Everybody else came from under a rock, but he didn't? It was an unfortunate chapter in America's history, but it set the stage for the war of today. Not in Afghanistan, nor Iraq, but right here in America.

This war escalated during the Clinton administration. The hate for the success of Bill and Hillary Clinton germinated into the Republican Revolution of 1994. The war on the poor was accelerated and culminated in the 1996 overhaul of welfare for poor people. TANF was created by the Personal Responsibility and Work Opportunity Act instituted under President Bill Clinton.

The Act provides temporary financial assistance while aiming to get people off of that assistance, primarily through employment. There is a maximum of 60 months of benefits within one's *lifetime*, but some states have instituted shorter periods. In enforcing the 60-month time limit, some states place limits on the adult portion of the assistance only, while still aiding the otherwise eligible children in the household. This was the death knell to Dr. Martin Luther King's "Poor Peoples Campaign." This ended the concept of holding America accountable.

Though politicians had enormous history in extra-marital affairs, President Clinton's Monica Lewinsky scandal gave ammunition to the conservative right's culture war. The setting for a "moral compass" was thrust upon anyone who wasn't them. Since Clinton had been unofficially throned as "America's First Black President," Blacks were made to apologize for any unwanton conduct—regardless of who caused it. Though the war was on, that standard seemed to avoid the very people calling for this newfound accountability: conservatives.

The terrorist attacks of September 11, 2001 gave the war license. Now, any person without Nordic features was fair game for racial profiling (formerly reserved for Black Americans). It was reason for Blacks to apologize to whites for *offending* them. All of the haunting racist divisions from Jim Crow were alive and well and fair game for the assault on anyone who happened to have pigmented skin.

More recently, following the re-election of President Obama, conservative commentator Bill O'Reilly lamented Obama's victory: "The white establishment is now the minority." He chalked up Obama's win to the majority of voters—Obama's majority—voted for the candidate that would "give them *stuff*." An insult to Black and brown people, where white presidents have been "giving them **stuff**" for the last 330 years!

In order for America to be strong, and for its populace to grow healthy, we must break down the walls of tradition that has caused us—many like me—to distrust and carry suspicion of members of the several other races and classes of this country.

Americans of any ilk must disassociate themselves from judgment of how people got where they are and rely solely on facts—especially regarding themselves. Most people "doing good" got there because of their parents and their skin pigmentation, period. Others lied, cheated and stole their way there. Some even slept their way to the middle class—and some to the top. Money is a determining factor in securing and maintaining freedom in a capitalist society. In that case, most of us won't have enough to be free. More than anything, people need to be honest; and as a condition of your freedom, you cannot apologize for being honest.

Chapter Ten

As A Condition of Your Freedom, You Cannot...
Renounce Violence

"I submit to you that if a man hasn't discovered something that he will die for, he isn't fit to live."
                                        --Martin Luther King, Jr.

Many will have heard of my writing and be directed to the book. You can't think that you can jump straight to chapter ten of this book and vilify me for calling for defending the redemption of oppressed peoples through violent means. One must have a full context of the call. The preceding nine chapters are equally as important as the last one. They work in concert.

The United States suffered a severe loss of its economic footing beginning in early 2007. It was in the forecast long before it hit the fan. Financial institutions were running wild as deregulation of financial instruments—and the industry as a whole— were quickly being dismantled.

Fiscal instability is the breeding ground for societal discord. When people are squeezed financially in a capitalist society, they get damned antsy. We saw this with the recession that Barack Obama inherited in 2009. Even he knew this elemental truth. He made the bold choice (or an unadvised one) to voice it:

You go into these small towns in Pennsylvania and, like a lot of small towns in the Midwest, the jobs have been gone now for 25 years and nothing's replaced them. And they fell through the Clinton administration, and the Bush administration, and each successive administration has said that somehow these communities are gonna regenerate and they have not.

And it's not surprising then they get bitter, they cling to guns or religion or antipathy toward people who aren't like them or anti-immigrant sentiment or anti-trade sentiment as a way to explain their frustrations.

These very people tried to get mad about the comment. They were stoked on by the conservative right—aiming for a war, a culture war. It was construed as an attack on NRA supporters and evangelicals—a strongly defined Republican voting bloc. Obama, who had no discernable flaws prior to this incident, now had the bullseye on his back. Unfortunately for America, he was right.

I wrote in my *Socially Speaking: The Other Side of the Tracks* commentary of November 1, 2009 about *"Obama's Prophecy"*:

Though we see the gun crimes of black males on TV—regardless if they are in simple possession or commit a drive-by—we rarely illuminate the consistent pattern of white, males angry about their fear of change...change in their financial status.

As a matter of fact, beginning in December '07, two separate shootings at church evangelical meetings occurred in Colorado Springs; "Cookie" Thornton shot & killed six people in a city council meeting on 2/7/08. From Southern California to Pembroke

Pines, Florida. 60 year-old Gordon Wheeler walked in armed a county board meeting in Little Falls, Minnesota, mad about his business finances and ended up dead, shot by police. Remember the man in Knoxville (the place I called home for 20 years) who walked into my friend's church and shot & killed two people at a children's program?

It appears from all fact and circumstance that President Obama was right. We've seen an angry bunch of [white] middle-class Americans. The many of those, think they run everything—and probably had. They've accused Obama of "trying to take their healthcare." We've seen them bring guns to rallies, get evangelically closer to God and fight for pro-gun legislation in districts where they don't even live. The political climate has changed since the election of Barack Obama...he's a prophet.

The following events of this nation saw the birth and rise of the Tea Party. Though they made all efforts to veil who they were, it was clear enough that Stevie Wonder could see it! White, male, evangelical, Protestant—with uncritical support for Israel and opposition to Barack Obama.

They attacked anyone who was different from them. The economic recession gave them license. President Obama, in all of his compromising political demeanor, only emboldened the Tea Party supporters.

Many candidates running for office during that time made statements and took positions that bordered on "fighting words." Many retractions were made, but the genie was out of the bottle...the damage had been done.

As an alternative to inaction, violence must always be on the table. It is a necessary means to problem solving. I further posit that violence is always to be a last resort. This is the unfortunate lesson of reality that America has taught us. Nothing is to be believed until some heads are busted.

The Utopian view

Martin Luther King, Jr., shared the hopes and dreams of many when he said, "I refuse to accept the view that mankind is so tragically bound to the starless midnight of racism and war that the bright daybreak of peace and brotherhood can never become a reality... I believe that unarmed truth and unconditional love will have the final word. "I think all men of the Black race want to be there. Unfortunately, whites won't allow it.

I do agree with King on the finality of this hope: that unarmed truth and unconditional love will have the final word...but that will be only after the head-busting and blood-letting has exhausted itself. There is no change without bloodshed—especially in a democracy like the United States of America.

"The hope of a secure and livable world lies with disciplined nonconformists who are dedicated to justice, peace and brotherhood." Martin Luther King, Jr., wanted what we all want, but know will never happen. Frederick Douglass said, "Power concedes nothing without a struggle." In the end, civil disobedience will spawn violent opposition. People in power never want to give up their power. So it has to be taken—and redistributed among the masses. Nothing else will do.

There are too many forces who usurp the ideals of justice, equality and liberty. As a result, the final solution is violence. Peace can come afterwards. Men of carnality only understand that. Just look at Israel. They subscribe to my theory—and the US backs it. I advocate for revolution. It would good if that revolution came in the form of cyber change, or peaceful sit-in, but those days are of days long gone.

Nelson Mandela

To break the creatively designed institution known as Apartheid, violence **had** to be on the table. Apartheid was a system of legal racial segregation enforced by the National Party government of South Africa between 1948 and 1994, under which the rights of the majority "non-white" inhabitants of South Africa were curtailed and minority rule by white people was maintained.

Apartheid was also practiced in South West Africa, under South African administration under a League of Nations mandate, until Namibian independence in 1990.

Racial segregation in South Africa began in colonial times. However, apartheid as an official policy was introduced following the general election of 1948.

New legislation classified inhabitants into racial groups ("black", "white", "colored", and "Asian"), and residential areas were segregated, sometimes by means of forced removals. From 1970, black people were deprived of their citizenship; legally becoming citizens of one of ten tribally based self-governing homelands called *Bantustans*, four of which became nominally independent states. The government segregated education, medical care, beaches, and other public services, and provided black people with services inferior to those of white people.

Apartheid sparked significant internal resistance and violence as well as a long trade embargo against South Africa. Since the 1950s, a series of popular uprisings and protests were met with the banning of opposition and imprisoning of anti-apartheid leaders. As unrest spread and became more violent, state organizations responded with increasing repression and state-sponsored violence. If I've said it once, I've said it a million times: as a condition of your freedom, you cannot renounce violence...heads must get busted and lives must be sacrificed. Otherwise, why would the oppressor change anything?

The white minority came up with ways to placate the restless natives. Reforms to apartheid in the 1980s failed to quell the mounting opposition, and in 1990 President Frederik Willem de Klerk began negotiations to end apartheid, culminating in multi-racial democratic elections in 1994, which were won by the African National Congress under Nelson Mandela. Only the threat of violence could facilitate real change.

For four days in August 2011, whites in England were nervous with anxiety as youths roamed the streets and exacted the worst havoc to hit England since World War II. This unrest wrecked the calm of the former empire.

The northwestern cities of Manchester and Liverpool, as well as Nottingham, Birmingham, West Bromwich and Wolverhampton, in the area of England known as the Midlands, saw the worst of the unrest during the capital's calm. Though the western media tried to sweep the cause under the rug and attribute the violence to "troublemakers" and "thugs," the unrest took place because of the great wealth disparity along the racial divide, sparked by the shooting of another young, Black man.

Henry Chu, reporter for the Seattle Times, saw what we all know, but whites in authority were not willing to let out of the bag: change needed to come.

The looting, arson and violence that killed five people sparked outrage over a "feral" underclass of mostly inner-city young people who gleefully plundered shops and destroyed livelihoods. Courts are working overtime to process hundreds of suspects, meting out harsh sentences as a deterrent, to widespread public approval.

A growing chorus, however, has begun pointing out that greed and contempt for the rules aren't just the preserve of the thugs who smashed store windows and helped themselves to plasma TVs and designer clothes.

These critics say the same cupidity and disregard for social responsibility also drove the bankers who awarded themselves big bonuses while peddling dubious financial products, the members of Parliament who bought expensive stereos or made lavish home improvements at taxpayer expense, the journalists who hacked into cellphones, the police officers who took bribes for information.

Many suburbs of London have an on-going (and hidden) history of police intrusions upon its black residents. Search and seizure on blacks ("stop-and-frisk" in the US), unemployment and job discrimination is rampant in Great Britain. This uncivil unrest comes as a direct result of disenfranchised residents feeling enough is enough. It's clear that if blacks are unemployed, then they want things to be equal. Now, after burning out businesses, there are many more white people unemployed along with them. I'd say that's an equalizer.

In the aftermath of the unrest, Great Britain began a re-tooling of its treatment of the poor. I am grieved that they focused on targeting the purported gangs of the urban communities, instead of the systemic, institutional problems at the core of the uprising. In turn, the authorities instituted an amnesty-like program, with social safety net-like features as a complement.

English authorities started Operation Connect in Waltham Forest, where a spasm of gang-related violence last summer, among other factors, encouraged the police to single out the borough for particular attention. The Connect process is for direct contact to be made with those people, either in person or in writing, and offer them the chance to "disengage" from gang life. This is a modified version of the "call ins" organized by the Boston Gun Project of the mid-1990s and, more recently, by Strathclyde police in Glasgow.

For those who do agree to a "diversion" plan – and around 50 people have done so thus far in Waltham Forest – an array of support services is on offer, ranging from help with employment and substance abuse, to housing re-location assistance for members and their families who feel they need to move as a part of the rupture. Still, none of that addresses systemic racism.

Although these services were needed a long time ago, none of this would've happened without violence. More is sure to come if whites keep the status quo. By the way, in January 2014, Despite being completely unarmed, a UK jury ruled by a majority of eight to two that 29-year-old Mark Duggan was lawfully killed by the police.

Martin King prophetically said, "A riot is the language of the unheard." Whites use language to demonize those seeking justice and equality. Stoking fear among the white majority by referring to those in revolt as "thugs," common practice among white men.

When I organized Knoxville's Black community in 2002 against police systematically killing Black men, then-Police Chief Phil Keith resorted to the old Southern language that usually scares white people: "Redd is nothing but a thug..." Now, this changes the conversation from the issue to the person. That's what authoritarians want...you to miss the issue.

Unfortunately, just as in America's civil rights movement, once Blacks felt all that could be won was, they got comfortable. My 30-year old baby sister just visited Durban, Cape Town, Johannesburg and other South African cities in December 2013. From what she shared with me, the vestiges of apartheid still shape South African politics and society today.

Strangely enough, when Nelson Mandela passed away in December of 2013, whites went to great efforts to emphasize his "conciliatory" nature. They found it imperative to stress that we focus on his call to forgiveness, as opposed to their actions that caused one to need to forgive. I found that insulting. That's an example of "revisionist history"...just leave out the good parts.

The Greek economic crisis of 2011

In early 2010, it was revealed that successive Greek governments had been found to have consistently and deliberately misreported the country's official economic statistics to keep within the monetary union guidelines. This had enabled Greek governments to spend beyond their means, while hiding the actual deficit from the EU overseers. This act is akin to Republicans in America who vehemently oppose government oversight; without it, they can steal the people's money liberally.

In May 2010, the Greek government deficit was again revised and estimated to be 13.6% which was one of the highest in the world relative to GDP and public debt was forecast, according to some estimates, to hit 120% of GDP during 2010, one of the highest rates in the world.

As a consequence, there was a crisis in international confidence in Greece's ability to repay its sovereign debt. The U.S. was headed in the same direction by the summer of 2011. In order to avert such a default, in May 2010 the other Eurozone countries, and the

International Monetary Fund (IMF) agreed to a rescue package which involved giving Greece an immediate €45 billion in bail-out loans, with more funds to follow, totalling €110 billion. In order to secure the funding, Greece was required to adopt harsh austerity measures to bring its deficit under control.

Here in America, the Republican caucused Tea Party members of Congress made their play to destroy the social safety net of the vast majority of America's under-class. Along with those measures, the security of America's middle class was also victimized by those conservative Republicans. They pushed the Obama administration to accept spending cuts—for the poor, which Obama said he wouldn't do—and never touched the richest of America in the form of tax hikes. Unlike Greece, America didn't act up.

The financial crisis—particularly the austerity package put forth by the EU and the IMF—has been met with anger by the Greek public, leading to riots and social unrest, while peaceful demonstrations have been taking place every evening in front of the Greek parliament since May 25, 2011.

On June 27th, trade union organizations commenced a forty-eight hour labor strike in advance of a parliamentary vote on the austerity package, the first such strike since 1974. Labor unions in the United States were so paralyzed, that they failed to do anything. This has been the case since the Reagan firing of striking Air Traffic Controllers in 1982.

Massive demonstrations were organized throughout Greece, intended to pressure parliament members into voting against the package. In Athens alone 38 arrests were made in addition to 75 people being detained, while 46 civilians and 38 policemen were injured. The second set of austerity measures was approved on June 29th, with 155 out of 300 members of parliament voting in favor. The vote had been seen as crucial for the country's future, as the EU and IMF had made future funding conditional on a positive outcome.

The masses were effectively made slaves by the ruling few. Again, white men stole the money. Violence had to be a part of the people's voice. They still got rolled like a ghetto drunk, but passivity is a non-seqiutor.

Arab spring 2011

The Arab Spring was a revolutionary wave of demonstrations and protests occurring in the Arab belt. I admit here, that this so-called "revolution" was manufactured and fostered by the United States and its western allies—for U.S. interests...mainly oil.

Beginning in December of 2010 there were revolutions in Tunisia and Egypt; a civil war in Libya; civil uprisings in Bahrain, Syria, and Yemen. Some heads had to get busted and lives were martyred; major protests in Algeria, Iraq, Jordan, Morocco, and Oman, as well as on the borders of Israel, and minor protests in Kuwait, Lebanon, Mauritania, Saudi Arabia, Sudan, and Western Sahara.

The protests shared elements of civil resistance in sustained campaigns involving strikes, demonstrations, marches and rallies, as well as the use of social media, such as Facebook, Twitter, and YouTube, to organize, communicate, and raise awareness in the face of state attempts at repression and internet censorship.

Demonstrations were also met with violent responses from authorities, as well as from pro-government militias and counter-demonstrators. What was most paradoxical was that the American-backed regimes acted like despots—with America's blessing—while America tried to play moral authority figure. Americans were stuck between the truth and the myth of American principle. Factually speaking, there is no such thing. That's why violence is the final arbiter of justice. All other factors fall in prior positions— including peace. Issues of democracy can only be settled at the business end of a rifle. That's the American way.

The Black Panthers

You want to talk about the surest way to get the power elite to negotiate. Fear is a hell of a motivator. The Black Panthers brought about the most acute change in America's racist status quo since Nat Turner's Rebellion 130 years earlier.

Began in 1966, the Black Panther Party achieved national and international notoriety through its involvement in the Black Power movement and in U.S. politics of the 1960s and 70s. The anti-racism agenda of that time is today considered one of the most significant social, political and cultural currents in U.S. history. The group's "provocative rhetoric, militant posture, and cultural and political flourishes permanently altered the contours of American

Identity." Simply put, the threat of head-busting and killing white people made negotiation a clear necessity. Who do you know *wants* their head busted?

Founded in Oakland, California, by Huey Newton and Bobby Seale on October 15, 1966, the organization initially set forth a doctrine calling primarily for the protection of African American neighborhoods from police brutality. They had the desire to "just get along" with whites, but of course, whites wanted no such thing. The attacks on the Black community had reached a plateau of unacceptability; a place where "being sick and tired of being sick and tired."

The organization's leaders espoused socialist and communist (largely Maoist) doctrines, however the Party's early black nationalist reputation attracted a diverse membership. Black Panther Party objectives and philosophy expanded and evolved rapidly during the party's existence. More relevant to the point, renouncing violence was not an option.

It took government subversiveness, unjust targeting, misinformation and co-opting of involved principles to quell the threat of opposition of people demanding their freedom and respect. Federal Bureau of Investigation Director J. Edgar Hoover called the party "the greatest threat to the internal security of the country," and he supervised an extensive program (COINTELPRO) of surveillance, infiltration, perjury, police harassment, assassination, and many other tactics designed to undermine Panther leadership, incriminate party members and drain the organization of resources and manpower. Through these tactics, Hoover hoped to diminish the Party's threat to the general power structure of the U.S., or even maintain its influence as a strong undercurrent. That's what fear looks like.

This type of fear was re-lived in the era following the 9/11 bombing. It takes violence as a reality in order to effect real change. Don't be surprised at my refrain: you cannot renounce violence as a condition of your freedom.

Unfortunately, I didn't make that up. That position long before I got here. It is a learned stand based on observation and experience within a tainted and hypocritical society. When people who control the economic resources of a country also advocate violent means to maintain that control, then one must be realistic. Violence is acceptable. If they say it, then it's free speech, if I say it, then its called terrorism.

Former South African President P.W. Botha told Nelson Mandela in 1985, that he could be a free man as long as he did one thing: publicly renounce violence. Mandela refused. That is why Mandela remained in prison until F.W. de Klerk freed him unconditionally.

There are white supremacists that to this day who despise de Klerk for that act. They accuse de Klerk of being an "appeaser." Factually speaking, South Africa was under pressure from the world community—to move into the future. Rights are never conceded without demand; peace is never gained without violence. Negotiations toward peace never come without the threat of violence. I didn't make that up, it's just history.

The bottom line is that Nelson Mandela never publicly renounced violence—and even today, after his death, whites see Mandela as a terrorist. That just shows me who the enemies of peace and the people truly are. It took violent insurgent acts to force the government to re-negotiate its long-standing position on civil and human rights. So who is really the terrorist?

Regarding the late-Mandela's position, its funny how, even American's admit that while armed resistance is justified in certain circumstances, violence threatens the processes of peaceful reform. Even in the early 90's, Nelson Mandela's stature was hoped to be used to preach a message of nonviolence and civil disobedience. Whites argued that Dr. King advocated nonviolence.

They held up the quote of Dr. King (yet they disrespected him during his lifetime), "The method of nonviolent resistance is effective in that it has a way of disarming opponents," Dr. King said. "It exposes their moral defenses, weakens their morale and at the same time works on their conscience. It makes possible for the individual to struggle for moral ends through moral means." In sharp contrast to Dr. King, Mr. Mandela continued to call for an "armed struggle." That was 1990.

Now, as history has played itself out, we have learned that Mandela was not only right, but a celebrated hero—for standing with "the people" over the interests of oligarchs: corporations, governments...terrorists.

The calls by neo-cons versus the call by me

At this point in history, we're seeing "culture wars" being conducted by extreme forces on the political Right. That is to say, they want to "take their country back." At political rallies during the 2010 campaign season, Tea Party supporters of this ideal showed up at rallies with guns slung over their shoulders. What was that symbolic of? They were saying, if we don't' win at the ballot box, we'll win it on the battlefield— the street.

I believe that we should not only take them seriously, but also take that page out of the American philosophy for change.

Don't get me wrong, I am pragmatic and honest about this ideal. Blacks are in the minority as far as population goes. But poor people aren't. A violent confrontation with the forces of oppression would mean that Blacks would lose as far as numbers go. It's sort of like the explanation the Dr. King gave in a 1965 *Playboy* interview on his view of Malcolm X's solution:

> *"I met Malcolm X once in Washington, but circumstances didn't enable me to talk with him for more than a minute. He is very articulate ... but I totally disagree with many of his political and philosophical views — at least insofar as I understand where he now stands. I don't want to seem to sound self-righteous, or absolutist, or that I think I have the only truth, the only way. Maybe he does have some of the answer. I don't know how he feels now, but I know that I have often wished that he would talk less of violence, because violence is not going to solve our problem. And in his litany of articulating the despair of the Negro without offering any positive, creative alternative, I feel that Malcolm has done himself and our people a great disservice. Fiery, demagogic oratory in the black ghettos, urging Negroes to arm themselves and prepare to engage in violence, as he has done, can reap nothing but grief."*

It's like there's no grief now? I don't believe in deferring grief in lieu of the grief you've got now. As I've said previously, oppressors will concede none of their power...and none of your grief.

What's wrong with America?

Look, I don't want to see fighting among any nation of people. That would be re-living the Civil War; there's no such thing as a "civil" war. I think there is no safer place to live and work than in the United States. Yet, it is till an unsafe place to live and work more so, if you're not white. That is problematic. Just ask Trayvon Martin or Renisha McBride. They were both killed by white men who lived in *self-induced perceived* fear.

There are militant-minded whites awaiting an uprising from Blacks that will give excuse to use their stockpiles of firearms. That's why they fiercely defend (and contort) the Second Amendment to the Constitution. That's why they battle so fiercely against background checks or tracking of gun purchases. It isn't government that they're really worried about...their desire is to annihilate and exterminate anyone who is not them.

That's why white conservatives are quick to frame uprisings for equality or human rights as "riots." Their adeptness at framing issues and incidents to scare Americans is a power tool. The late Martin Luther King, Jr. was a prophet who saw today's Tea party coming. "The more there are riots, the more repressive action will take place, and the more we face the danger of a right-wing takeover and eventually a fascist society." That's where we are today.

Right-wing conservatives masquerade as Republicans, chiefly because there aren't many options in a two-party political system country. Libertarians like former Rep. Ron Paul of Texas know that. That's why he always ran as a Republican (though I acknowledge, his first run for president was as a Libertarian).

The aim is to disenfranchise every other race of people as to reclaim their superior status of the early part of America's history. "Taking Our Country Back" is the motto embraced by the Tea Party when they formed in 2009...they just needed something to galvanize against. Barack Obama was that something.

One of my favorite political scientists, George Lakoff, recounts the history of this latest assault on American progress:

> Back in the 1950's conservatives hated each other. The financial conservatives hated the social conservatives. The libertarians did not get along with the social conservatives or the religious conservatives. And many social conservatives were not religious. A group of conservative leaders got together around William F. Buckley Jr. and others and started asking what the different groups had in common and whether they could agree to disagree in order to promote a general conservative cause. They started magazines and think tanks, and invested millions of dollars.

> The first thing they did, their first victory, was getting Barry Goldwater nominated in 1964. He lost, but when he lost, they went back to the drawing board and put more money into organization. During the Vietnam War, they noticed that most of the bright young people in the country were not becoming conservatives. *Conservative* was a dirty word. Therefore, in 1970, Lewis Powell, just two months before he became a Supreme Court justice appointed by Nixon (at the time, he was chief counsel to the U.S. Chamber of Commerce), wrote a memo—the Powell Memo. It was a fateful document. He said that the conservatives had to keep the country's best and brightest young people from becoming anti-business. What we need to do,

Powell said, is to set up institutes within the universities and outside the universities. We have to research, we have to write books, we have to endow professorships to teach these people the right way to think.

After Powell went to the Supreme Court, these ideas were taken up by William Simon...he convinced some very wealthy people—Coors, Scaife, Olin—to set up the Heritage Foundation, the Olin professorships, the Olin Institute at Harvard, and other institutions. These institutes have done their jobs very well...the conservatives support their intellectuals. They create media opportunities. They have media studios down the hall in institutes so that getting on television is easy. Eighty percent of the talking heads on television are from the conservative think tanks. Eighty percent.[28]

We've yet to recover from that organizing. The conservatives have strategized so effectively, as to pervade every step we take; every issue we vision. Nothing is sacred nor protected from attack. From redistricting to voting rights, from immigration to climate change, from consumer protections to judicial appointments, from workplace regulations to financial industry oversight, every argument is about "taking their country back," the mind-framing that George Lakoff talked about in "*Don't Think of an Elephant*" is prevalent rather than the reality of the issue itself. This has caused a retardation of progress for minority and working class Americans. That prohibition of progress can only be snapped by confrontation and persistence.

Confrontation doesn't have to, but usually brings violence. That's why the holders of the nation's resources pay law enforcement well, don't mess with their unions and constantly pat them on the back; as law enforcement protects their holdings, lifestyles and traditions. Just look at Egypt during the so-called "Arab Spring" or America's Occupy Wall Street.

The Final Analysis

What I know is that, just like the United States' foreign policy position(s) against Iran, North Korea, China and any other adversarial nations of people, the threat of violence keeps violence at bay. I'm not for words of aggression, nor am I for saber-rattling; one must be prepared to respond. Those of us who want peace, **must** be peaceable. I advocate for peace and peaceable tactics...**and** violence is not off the table.

We learned immensely from the struggle of Nelson Mandela and the South African break with apartheid. The threat of violence has, and always will, come from the authority figure in any American equation. From the invent of the Klu Klux Klan to the 1921 Tulsa Bombing; from the Selma Bus Boycotts to Kent State, from the Attica massacre to the Oscar Grant murder, we *know* who the aggressor is—and more importantly, why.

If there is no resistant threat of action, then the authority figure has no reason to negotiate with you— much less, concede anything to you.

The bottom line is, you cannot ignore the underlying problem and expect it to get fixed. You cannot trust that the one in power will remedy that problem. If keeping the problem in place benefits him, then why would he fix it? You cannot settle for crumbs off the table and live as happy as he. If you believe what you are demanding is right, fair and just—and can prove that it is—you cannot compromise that stand.

Furthermore, you must not allow yourself to become fatigued; it is too easy to quit. Then you'll be right back where you began, oppressed. If you brought it up, then it must have credence; you cannot sit on the sidelines and expect things to change. You can pray about it, but prayer alone never got anything done. Somebody must act on what the Creator has provided. You cannot be a coward in the face of evil; the oppressor banks on that. They may even talk to you, but you can't talk it to death. Injustice is never a long conversation.

In the final analysis, as a condition of your freedom, you cannot make apologies for offending, affronting, demanding, nor antagonizing an unjust system when seeking justice, equality and/or fairness. It is what it is; no amount of appeasement will ever make an oppressed party whole. In all of that, peace is never achieved without the real possibility of conflict. Violent conflict must always remain on the periphery as means to the end for a peaceful calm...if you choose to be free.

Index

Biblography

1. Foreword-"The Invention of the White Race" by Theodore Allen

2. Foreword-"Theodore Allen's The Invention of the White Race," article by Jefferey Perry http://www.zcommunications.org/theodore-w-allen-s-the-invention-of-the-white-race-by-jeffrey-b-perry

3. Chptr 1-Eugenics Popularization essay; Seldon, Steve, University of Maryland; http://www.eugenicsarchive.org/html/eugenics/essay6text.html

4. Chptr 1- "Wealth Gap Rise to Record Highs..." -Kochar, Fry and Taylor; Pew Research, Social and Demographic Trends report, July 26, 2011

5. Chptr 1-Ben Bernanke comment: Race, Wealth and Intergenerational Poverty" by Darrick Hamilton. http://prospect.org/article/race-wealth-and-intergenerational-poverty

6. Chptr 1- "Stuff White Girls Say,": Tell Me More (NPR), Michelle Martin, January 12, 2012

7. Chptr 1- "Presidential Pardons Heavily Favor Whites," ProPublica report, Linzer and LaFluer, December 3, 2011

8. Chptr 3- "Genetics and Criminal Behavior,"-The Diane Rhem Show (NPR), June 23, 2011

9. Chptr 4-de Tocqueville, Alexis. *Democracy in America* (1840), part 2, page 36: "The position of the Americans is therefore quite exceptional, and it may be believed that no other democratic people will ever be placed in a similar one."

10. Chptr 6- "Wealth Gap Widens Between US Whites, Minorities"-US Census data, July 26, 2011

11. Chptr 6-G. William Domhoff, Power In America, on-line article, January 2011: http://sociology.ucsc.edu/whorulesamerica/power/wealth.html

12. Chptr. 6-Avery, Robert B.; Rendall, Michael S. (2002), *Lifetime Inheritances of Three Generations of Whites and Blacks*, 107, The University of Chicago Press

13. Chptr. 6-Keister, Lisa A. (2004), *Race, Family Structure, and Wealth: The Effect of Childhood Family on Adult Asset Ownership*, 47, University of California Press

14. Chptr 8- Burr, Charles R. "A Brief History of Anacostia, Its Name, Origin, and Progress", *Records of the Columbia Historical Society*, 1920.

15. Chptr 9-"Time to Kill Hamp" by Kevin D. Williamson, National Review On-Line, March 3, 2011http://www.nationalreview.com/articles/261152/time-kill-hamp-kevin-d-williamson

16. Chprt 9-"swiss Bankers Charged in $1.2 Billion Fraud" by james O' Toole @ CNN Money, January 3, 2012http://money.cnn.com/2012/01/03/news/swiss_bankers_charged/index.htm?hpt=hp_t2

17. Chptr 10-Brennan Center, "Voting Laws Changes in 2012" http://www.brennancenter.org/content/resource/voting_law_changes_in_2012/

18. Chptr 10-Steve Jobs, CBS News 60 minutes; Walter Issacson. http://www.cbsnews.com/video/watch/?id=7385704n

19. Chptr 10-"Poverty Stuck at 15%, 46.5 Million" by Hope Yen, AP, September 17, 2013http://bigstory.ap.org/article/analysts-2012-poverty-rate-show-slight-decline

20. Chptr 10-"Black Panther Party". Encyclopædia Britannica. http://www.britannica.com/eb/article-9015498/Black-Panther-Party. Retrieved March 27, 2008.

21. Chptr 10-"*Don't Think of An Elephant: Know Your Values and Frame the Debate*". Chelsea Green, 2004 http://www.chelseagreen.com/bookstore/item/elephant

Endnotes

[1]"*Lies My Teacher Told Me*" by James Loewen
[2] Race Wealth and Intergenerational Poverty, Darrick Hamilton and William Darity, Jr., *Mother Jones*, September 16, 2009
[3] DC Schools Have the Largest Black-White Achievement Gap in Federal Study by Lyndsey Layton, December 6, 2011.
http://www.washingtonpost.com/local/education/dc-schools-have-largest-black-white-achievement-gap-in-federal-study/2011/12/06/gIQArNnMcO_story.html

[4]"Presidential Pardons Heavily Favor Whites" by Dafner Linzer and Jennifer LaFluer. December 3, 2011http://www.propublica.org/article/shades-of-mercy-presidential-forgiveness-heavily-favors-whites
[5]"That's Racist" NPR story by NedaUlaby, June 27, 2011http://www.npr.org/blogs/monkeysee/2011/06/27/137451481/thats-racist-how-a-serious-accusation-became-a-commonplace-quip
[6]Glenn Becks claims President Obama is "a racist" on Fox News, July 28, 2009. http://www.youtube.com/watch?v=2K8R2PDmbmA
[7]The Slave Trade Compromise, The US Constitution. http://en.wikipedia.org/wiki/Constitutional_Convention_(United_States)
[8]"Stuff White Girls Say: Funny of Offensive?" by Michelle Martin, NPR, January 12, 2012. http://m.npr.org/story/145101169
[9]"Love your enemies…" quote from Jesus, Holy Bible, Luke 6:27
[10] Instructions to Census Enumerators on race determination by census year. http://usa.ipums.org/usa/voliii/tEnumInstr.shtml
[11] "Genetics and Criminal Behavior," The Diane Rhem Show, NPR, June 23, 2011. http://thedianerehmshow.org/shows/2011-06-23/genetics-and-criminal-behavior
[12] "Israel Ramps UpCampaign AgainstGaza Aid Flotilla," Washington Post, June 28, 2011. http://www.washingtonpost.com/world/israel-ramps-up-campaign-against-gaza-aid-flotilla/2011/06/28/AG59dbpH_story.html
[13] "The New Jim Crow: Mass Incarceration in the Age of Colorblindness" by Michelle Alexander. http://www.newjimcrow.com/
[14]"Buffalo High School Basketball Team Suspended After Using Racial Slur," New York Daily News, by Nina Mandell, December 9, 2011. http://articles.nydailynews.com/2011-12-09/news/30500363_1_racial-slur-girls-basketball-team-racial-allegations
[15] "Homeland: Immigration in America" PBS special, July 20, 2012. http://www.pbs.org/destinationamerica/usim.html
[16] G. William Domhoff, Power In America, on-line article, January 2011: http://sociology.ucsc.edu/whorulesamerica/power/wealth.html

[17]"Lifetime Inheritances of Three Generations of Whites and Blacks." American Journal of Sociology, 2002 by Avery, Robert B. and Michael S. Rendall. www.npc.umich.edu/news/events/early_life/.../conley.doc
[18] "Wealth Gaps Rise to Record Highs Between Whites, Blacks, Hispanics" by Rakesh Kochhar, Richard Fry and Paul Taylor, PewResearchCenter, July 26, 2011. http://www.pewsocialtrends.org/2011/07/26/wealth-gaps-rise-to-record-highs-between-whites-blacks-hispanics/
[19] "New Yorkers Back Occupy Wall Street Protestors, Poll Shows" by Esme Deprez, Bloomberg News, October 17, 2011
[20]"The Best Way to Rob a Bank Is to Own One: How Corporate Executives and Politicians Looted the S&L Industry" by William K. Black, University of Texas Press, 2005
[21] "Officers Resist Group's Plan to Tape Police Activities" by J.J. Stambaugh, February 18, 2002, Knoxville News-Sentinel, A1
[22]"Slavery By Another Name: The Re-Enslavement of Black People in America from the Civil War to World War II" by Douglas Blackmon, 2008, Doubleday
[23] "The Immortal Life of Henrietta Lacks" by Rebecca Skloot, 2011, Crown
[24] "Voting Law Changes in 2012" by Wendy R. Weiser and Lawrence Norden, The Brennan Center publication, October 3, 2011

[25]"10 Million Hispanics Could Be Affected by State Voter I.D. Laws , Study Says" by The Christian Science Monitor, September 24, 2012,quoting study by The Advancement Project

[26] "Wealth Gap Between Whites and Minorities in U.S. Widens" by Global Post, July 26, 2011

[27] *Culture Wars: The Struggle to Define America"* by James Davison Hunter, BasicBooks, 1991

[28]"Don't Think of an Elephant! Know Your Values and Frame the Debate" by George Lakoff; Chelsea Green Publishing, 2004, pp.15-16

ABOUT THE AUTHOR

Perry Redd, *longtime activist, community organizer & political operative, is the Executive Director of the workers rights advocacy, Sincere Seven, and author of the syndicated socio-political column, "The Other Side of the Tracks." He is also the host of the internet-based talk radio show, Socially Speaking, in Washington, DC. Redd is also a prolific singer/ songwriter writing and recording well over 2,500 compositions.*